ON THE ROAD

LINDA CHADWICK

ON THE ROAD

A TEXAS GROUPIE'S MEMOIR

PALMETTO
P U B L I S H I N G
Charleston, SC
www.PalmettoPublishing.com

Paperback ISBN: 979-8-8229-3204-3
eBook ISBN: 979-8-8229-3205-0

Many thanks and all my love to my wonderful husband.
You are the man of my dreams, Doug.
Many thanks and all my love to my unbelievable children
Amber & Zachary.
And to Debbie—I wouldn't have wanted to share these
adventures with anyone else.

"Striking a perfect balance between naivete and knowing, Linda's storytelling will enchant."
—Dev Scott Flores (Debbie)

Contents

Introduction

The things I can do.

I have sat down with pen and paper so many times, trying to garner the courage to write it all down, every exciting detail that has happened throughout my life.

I was just a starry-eyed young girl with my head permanently in the clouds, full of make-believe and fantasy. I probably had enough dreams to share with one hundred girls. I might not have been a popular girl, but I had no doubt in my mind that I was definitely very special.

One day it was as if I stepped through a magical doorway and right into all my dreams coming true. It was me, actually a part of it all. I remember the excitement of standing backstage with a laminated VIP pass dangling around my neck, a pass that was given to me by the musician standing in front of twenty thousand people—twenty-thousand people that only dreamed that they could be standing in my place and envied me as I walked by. It was a feeling I would never take for granted, and I would remain so thankful to be just a page of rock and roll history.

I remember sitting in that old mulberry tree in my backyard with my pen and paper, writing my make-believe stories, closing my eyes with dreams of how I wished to be and all the things I could do.

Oh yea…The things I could do.

It's a Groupie!

I took my first breath on July 28, 1963. There wasn't anything out of the ordinary about my arrival on this earth. To say the least, you could say I was a very welcome surprise. The chronological sequence of my birth made me the last child, the baby of the family. I had two older siblings. My brother Terry was ten years older than I. My brother Randy was eight years older than I. My mother experienced complications stemming from my brother Randy's childbirth, and the physician explained she would not be able to conceive again. Eight years later my parents received an unexpected surprise. "It's a groupie!"

Mom would finally have her little girl to dress in frilly dresses and tie hair bows in her blond hair. My father would be blessed with another little girl to cuddle and bounce on his knee. Yeah, you caught that, didn't you? My father was married once before but tragically lost his wife and three-year-old daughter in an automobile accident. I in no way replaced his daughter Carolyn. In fact I became a part of that family. I considered her the sister I always wanted. I loved her from the moment I understood who she was. Recently, I was watching a home movie. In the movie, I must have been two or three years old, and I was carrying around a photograph of Carolyn.

So there I was, probably the most spoiled and overly protected child that may have ever existed. Everyone described me as a very friendly and bubbly child. My mother made sure

I never wanted for anything. She was extremely creative in making clothes for me and all my dolls, and once she even made me a Barbie doll house that took up a whole room. Most of my playtime activities were indoors because I was a very fragile and weak child, allergic to grass and just about every stinging, biting bug that existed. I had a terrible reaction once to the dastardly asp caterpillar, which exists only in Texas.

My father was a carpenter and a very hardworking man. He wore old-fashioned Dickies striped overalls, with all the tools he used attached to the utility loops and in every pocket handfuls of sawdust. The smell of sawdust was a comfort to me and meant my daddy was near. My first and warmest memory of my father is when he would come home from work. He would immediately begin to seek me out. "Where's my little girl?" I was very little, and he would gently toss me on the bed, tickling me and rolling me back and forth. I just remember giggling like crazy, and the next day it would happen all over again. My father always made time for me, even when he began to get older and wasn't feeling well. We would always play Ping-Pong or toss the ball or the Frisbee. He was even the coach of my Youth Association softball team, the Green Giants. My father was so affectionate that it was hard to believe that he came from a not-so-affectionate family. He used to tell me of times his mother and father would just pick up and go out of town, leaving him and his brothers to fend for themselves. Shockingly, he told me his mother had never outwardly said "I love you" to him or his brothers. I couldn't imagine, having grown up surrounded by love. It wasn't until my grandmother was in a nursing home that it became clear to me. We were getting ready to leave when Grandma reached for his hand and said, "Love you a little, love you a lot—I love you like a little pig." In my mind I couldn't help but think, "What the fuck!!??" What the hell was that even supposed to mean? Daddy smiled and seemed quite content with that.

My parents always made sure I had animals to play with, mostly dogs. My first pet was a black poodle named Sugar. She was an inside dog with one very odd idiosyncrasy that soon made her an outdoor dog. When it was time to make a bowel movement, she would back her ass up against the wall and take the shit. Sergeant Pepper was a black-and-white mutt that really meant a lot to me. He was with me through my very painful and awkward teenage years. He knew when I was upset, and he would stand at attention, counseling, and listen to my every word.

Christmas holidays were magical to me when I was little, and I remember most of them so vividly. Christmas was a chaotic event from start to finish. Mom and Dad would pack the car up with all the gifts and food, heading to my cousin Ioni's house. I thought Ioni was so beautiful, and I looked up to her. She was a heavyset woman; she would fix her hair and put on a full face of makeup with brightly colored lipstick. It was always a huge feast. She was a phenomenal cook. After we ate, everyone moved to the Christmas tree, where the hysteria of unwrapping gifts ensued. No matter how tired we all were, we would load up and go to Nanie's house to open all her presents. At the end of the night, we would head back to our house. When I was little, it was all about making Santa Claus seem as real as possible to me. My family was really good at it, and my parents would even secretly enlist my brothers. It wasn't until I was grown that I figured out the truth, and I am not entirely proud of that. There was one Christmastime in particular that no matter how hard I tried, I could not figure out how my parents did it. Santa Claus had to be real! So as an adult, I finally asked my brother Terry, "How did they do it?" My brother laughed and began to explain, "Mom and Dad didn't do it. Randy and I did it all." He went on to explain that before we left for Ioni's house, my dad leaned into the back seat and told my brothers to go back into the house to get his cigarettes. That is when it all went down. He said Daddy already had all the gifts assembled, hidden in another room, and all they had to do was quickly set it all up, then head back to the car with Daddy's pack of cigarettes. So there it all was—when we arrived back home that night, Santa Claus had come. Like I said, it was truly magical.

Easter was another memorable event. My mother would make sure I had a beautiful Easter dress with matching bonnet, shoes, and purse. We would go to church and afterward hunt for Easter eggs with all the other children. I can remember not wanting the day to end, so Mom and Dad would continue to hide eggs in our living room until bedtime. When I was little, my family attended a really wonderful church with a very vibrant pastor. His name was Dan, and his family presented me with my very first Bible. This was back in a more innocent time, when churches were good to be a part of and actually meant something.

Whenever we needed clothes or shoes, Mom would load us up and take us to downtown Fort Worth. We didn't have malls or strip malls like we do now. Leonard Brothers Department Store had everything you could ever need. On the sidewalk corners, people with disabilities would perform for money. There was an old blind man and woman, and they would play guitar and sing while shaking a can, begging for money. There was also a man who didn't have any legs. He would sit in a wooden box with wheels, and he would use his hands to push himself around. He would also beg for money. I was very frightened by them and would grasp tightly to my mother's hand or clothing. My mom would always put money in their cans, and then we would head into the store. The huge appeal of Leonard Brothers Department Store for every kid in Fort Worth was Toyland. There are really no words to explain just how amazing this place was. Toyland was on its own floor, and you had to ride the elevator to get to it. The doors would open, and every child's eyes would glaze over in sheer wonderment. Christmastime was different, especially if you were one of those kids (like me) who was terrified of sitting in Santa Claus's lap. When those elevator doors opened, Santa Claus would be the first thing you would see, and the screaming would begin. Parents would push, scurrying their children past so the screaming would subside, knowing every one of those children would be forced into Santa Claus's lap for the obligatory screaming-kid picture. Yeah, we all got one tucked away in the family pictures.

During my childhood, it was such an innocent time. You didn't have to be afraid of people like you do now. My childhood was picture perfect to me. Flashbacks of memories flood my mind. As I got older, I began to play outside more. I was seeking privacy and alone time. Mom would let me ride my bicycle to my friend's house to play. I loved my bicycle! Metallic purple, banana seat, and fringe dangling from the handlebar grips. I was the legendary Evil Knievel of my neighborhood, jumping off large hills and going into slides. Riding my bicycle was so much fun, and it gave me the freedom I was seeking. It was all well and good, but all things must come to an end. It happened…my major bicycle accident where I would go down in flames. I was riding my bicycle home, taking a sharp right, headed straight for my driveway, when all of a sudden my wheels hit a patch of gravel. It was at that moment I knew I was in trouble, and my body braced for the worst possible scenario. The bicycle wheels lost contact with the street, and so did I. For that fleeting moment, I knew what it was like to fly. I literally flew through the air, and when I saw where my body was about to land, panic ensued. I landed in a huge patch of prickly cactus in our neighbor's yard. Our neighbor was an elderly man, and he was sitting by his front window watching the whole event unfold. Everyone came running. I remember our neighbor yelling, "Oh my God, she's dead!!" It was at that point that I do not remember anything. Afterward, I was painfully sore and really beat up but luckily had no broken bones. The best thing about the accident was that I became quite a legend in my neighborhood, even with the boys, and in my world I would take whatever fame I could get.

I didn't have my own bedroom and wouldn't until I was nearly a teenager. I slept on a little cot right beside my parents' bed, and at night my mom would hang her arm off the side of the bed with her hand on me at all times. I also didn't have my own chair at the dinner table until I was a teenager. I sat in my high chair. Okay, I was a very small-framed child—no judgments!! It worked until the hierarchy shifted and one of my brothers moved out on his own.

Dinnertime was never boring at our house, especially when my brothers were living at home. Terry was the cool dude, but Randy had deemed himself the black sheep of the family and played the part quite well in his black-rimmed glasses. Terry called them serial killer glasses. It could get rather heated between the two of them, as they continued to add jabs and insults to an already festering pot. Mom would try to referee as best she could, while beads of sweat would continue to form across Randy's forehead. Me? I was pretty smart. I wouldn't get involved. I watched. I observed. I learned. Mostly I anticipated when it would all come to a head. That was when the fun would begin. Terry was out to push all Randy's buttons tonight as he flicked pieces of scrambled eggs at Randy's face. Randy glared at Terry. "You better stop." It was going well for Terry until a piece of egg actually hit him on his eyeglasses. In the blink of an eye, IT WENT DOWN! I was a little girl, but I can remember this clearly, as if it happened yesterday. Food began flying. Then suddenly Randy hurled a fork. It impaled Terry's chest! Yes! A fork! It was at this point I either passed out or sank underneath the dinner table for protection. I have some sort of mental block about the event. I am sure Daddy probably exploded with his once-a-year "GODDAMNIT!!!" and Mom (in her sweetest voice) calmed everyone down and cleaned everything up and of course removed the fork from Terry's chest. No stitches needed.

In seeking more privacy, I discovered there was a huge mulberry tree that I could climb quite effortlessly. It had a crook that curved, creating the perfect perch for me to safely straddle. I also constructed a rope pulley system that could bring my books and writing utensils up to me. I would spend hours sitting up in that tree reading my Nancy Drew books, unaware that I was developing a lifelong passion for writing. I would daydream of a life that existed far away from the crook in that tree. Poetry was my penchant. I began writing words that were far beyond my innocent years of ten or eleven years old. I never believed that my words would amount to much. I thought they were just a pastime, getting me from point A to point B. In my early twenties, however, I was awarded a Fort Worth literary award. It was a group of older, educated intellectuals standing up and saying "Linda Temple actually has talent," and let me tell you—it fucking felt like an Academy Award to me.

Morphine

My mom, Marjorie was born in 1931 and died in 2004. She lived her early years in the shadow of her older brother. She was absolutely beautiful and had what it took to become a Hollywood starlet. When she was a teenager, she was approached by an authentic Hollywood agent in Fort Worth while walking with her friends down the sidewalk. The agent tried to convince her, with a legitimate contract in hand, to leave for a world of fame and fortune. Sixteen years old, my mother smiled, already knowing what she really wanted for herself, so she politely declined his offer. Her dreams were to become a wife and mother. She had no shortage of suitors, but she had eyes only for one, and it was my father. I loved hearing how they met over and over. My father had a date with the girl up the street, and Mom found out about it. She prepared for the ultimate chess move, getting dressed in a pair of shorts and a button-up shirt tied at the waist. She hurried outside, perching herself on a large concrete fixture in her front yard. You have to understand something before I go on…My mother was a long and lean 5'10" in stature, with beautiful long legs. She was impossible to miss, and as my father drove by, it was like a clip from a Looney Tunes cartoon with his eyes bulging out. "Your daddy saw me, went and canceled the date with the other girl, and then came back to take me out," she would tell me. Checkmate, I'd say. My parents were married in Decatur,

Texas, in 1949. They purchased a nice piece of property in the Sansom Park addition and with a small loan began building their home with their own two hands. My mom explained that once one loan was paid off, they would go and get another, building more and more until they had a comfy home.

My mother worked throughout our childhood. I can remember her working at a candy company, at a department store, at a five-and-dime, and as a lunchroom lady, and she even owned a few businesses of her own. My mother would work all day and still manage to take perfect care of her home, her husband, and her children. I wouldn't understand where all her energy came from and just how tired she truly was until I became a wife and mother. She also managed to be a room mother for all our school classes and also took on extra activities, such as being a Girl Scout Bluebird leader. She was a great mother, teaching us the Bible, morals, and values. There was never a moment that we didn't exist within a foundation of love and understanding. Unfortunately, there were dark times to come, realizations we would discover in the upcoming years that would leave us all in a state of disbelief. Our mother was a pillar of strength that we all depended on, counted on, and there was nothing she couldn't do and no problem that she couldn't solve.

It was I who first suspected that something was wrong. My father had never been very healthy, but his health had begun to deteriorate more and more. He and I were walking together in the backyard when he said he wanted to talk about something important. "Your mother isn't well." My heart sank as he continued. "Once I am gone, I want you to promise me you and your brothers will look after her." I did not want to hear what he was saying, nor did I even understand. Mom had always had everything under control. Dad's health continued to go down until he fell into a coma-like state. Mom sat by him, begging for him not to leave her. It was the hardest thing I ever witnessed. Daddy passed away, and our pillar of strength began to crumble right before our eyes. First her mental health and then her physical health began to diminish. My mother did not want to live in this world anymore without my father. At the end, hospice approached, counseled us, and explained that they would be with us through the transition to the very end. I stayed by her side as they administered repeated dose after dose of morphine, escorting my mother to her very last breath.

"What a strong heart she had," the nurse said.

I swallowed hard as my tears rolled down my cheeks. "You have no idea." I was with my mother as I came into this world, and I was with her when her beautiful soul left this world. FUCKING MORPHINE!

Forget About It

My Daddy, Glen was born in 1927 and he died in 2002. How can I describe my daddy better than saying he was the best man I have ever had in my life? He was a debonair-looking young man. He was an exceptionally skilled carpenter; in fact, he built the furniture in Elvis Presley's private Learjet, the Lisa Marie. My father never really had things easy in life, but you would never hear him complain.

Times were very difficult in his youth. His parents were trying to raise three young boys through the Depression, but then his father broke his back, leaving his mother as the sole provider for the family. Tragedy struck when one of his brothers was run over by a police car and killed. His mother was diagnosed with breast cancer and survived. There were times his parents would leave on vacations, leaving the boys home to fend for themselves. My father would tell me stories about how he and his brother would ride off on their horses, camping and hunting for their own food. He would tell me he loved sneaking through gardens, picking and eating vegetables. He said warm tomatoes were his favorite. He said he also started smoking when he was eight years old by peeling tree bark off and rolling it up. My father could tell some really tall tales, and many would question the validity of the stories, but I knew they were all true. It all sounded like wonderful adventures to me, but the truth is, none of us will ever really know how hard the times really were on him.

My father, by twenty years old, had already lived a whole other lifetime before any of us were even glimmers in his eyes. He was married once before, and they had a three-year-old baby named Carolyn. She and my father's first wife were tragically killed in an automobile accident. I was the first person from our family to read the horrific newspaper article about the terrible events that occurred that day. My grandmother gave it to me one day while I was staying at her house. She said, "Someone needed to read and know." I sat silently on her couch reading it to myself, the explicit detail. At first, it felt as if it were an intrusion into a part of my dad's life I shouldn't know about. Tears rolled down my cheeks

How could this be my daddy? How could he have gone on with his life and survived such a devastating tragedy? It just seemed so surreal. I eventually mustered up enough courage to approach him with the article. "Grandma gave it to me."

He sat back and began to explain it all to me in his own words while holding tightly to the aged article. "It was an argument," he said. My father worked for a minor-league baseball team called the Fort Worth Cats. In that time, minor-league baseball was just as popular as the major leagues. They asked him to accompany them out on the road. He was thrilled, considering it to be an honor. His wife, Doris, did not feel the same way, and they fought about it. She dropped him off at the ballpark and quickly left, driving too fast during a rainstorm. Then the inevitable happened. She lost control of the car, swerving and hitting a telephone pole, which killed her instantly. The baby was thrown several feet from the car and died upon arrival at the emergency room. My father shared this part of his life with me, and I felt honored. I would always cherish his memories of Doris and Carolyn.

My father always seemed to be suffering from some sort of illness and complained of feeling bad most of the time. When he felt good, there wasn't anything he couldn't do. I loved him so much, and there has never been another man in my life that could measure up to the man he was. After he died, my mother gave me a ziplock baggie with one of his T-shirts sealed airtight, and every now and then I would unzip it ever so slightly just to be able to smell that comforting smell of my daddy.

Mom and Dad had a very loving relationship, married sixty plus years. They laughed. They sang. They shared a whole lifetime together. After both of my parents were gone, I prayed for some sort of sign that they were now together. That prayer was answered through my dream. There he was, so handsome and healthy, standing in front of the garage. He looked at me and smiled, and the warmth of his smile engulfed me. "We are together and happy."

He Bought Me a Horse!

My brother Terry was born in 1952.

In every television show and every movie, there is always one house where all the kids congregate. That was our house, the cool house. There was always a water hose to grab a cool drink from on a hot summer day, and as long as you got home before the streetlamp came on, all was right with the world.

My brothers had loads of friends, and all their bicycles would be strewn all over the driveway, and as the years went by the bicycles were replaced by cool cars and pickup trucks. Daddy would teach all the guys how to do all the minor and major upkeep. My dad and brothers could disassemble a whole car and have it put back together *and* running by sunset. There might be one or two rogue bolts left.

My brothers were ten and eight years older than I was, so they had pretty much graduated from the cradle of adolescence and were at the precipice of adulthood by the time I entered the world. They experienced freedom! I was childishly jealous and sometimes wished I could disappear with them down below the hills of Marion Sansom Park's Inspiration Point. I could only imagine the fun they were having building forts and battling wild animals and the watery rapids of the dam.

Remember me saying that my father was the best man I ever had in my life? Well, my brother Terry would be the second best.

I honestly think I must have loved him the moment I laid eyes on him.

My brother and I always had a great relationship, never fighting or angry at each other. I knew growing up that if I ever needed anything, I could count on him. Terry is just one of those types of people that everyone knows or wants to know. If you come to him as a stranger, you will leave as his friend and can rest assured that if you ever need him, he will be there.

I remember one day in particular when I was about eight years old. I was playing outside. I wasn't sure if what I saw was real or not, but as it got closer, my heart leaped with joy. It was my brother Terry driving home in his city truck, and in the back of the truck was a real live no-shit Shetland pony! My brother had brought me home a pony!! This was possibly every little girl's dream come true, and my big brother saw that mine came true.

As I grew older, Terry's and my biggest connection was music. He was my teacher, and I was his muse. He always had impeccable taste in music, and my mind absorbed everything he taught me. He would have the newest and most ultimate stereo sound systems. He would blast the music so loud you could almost feel your soul vibrating within your body. Every now and then, I was allowed to go into his room, and he would play music for me. Of course with one rule: "Don't look up." He'd grin. I agreed, but when he wasn't looking, I looked up. Big-boobed naked ladies plastered all over his ceiling. I would giggle, then get back to listening to Frank Zappa, the Moody Blues, Pink Floyd, and more.

Terry has been an amazing brother throughout my entire life, and it's even more amazing the older we get. He will always be a huge puzzle piece that completes me.

The Black Sheep

My brother Randy was born in 1955.

It seems that from the moment I was born, Randy had an untamable animosity toward me. I asked my brother Terry once, "Why doesn't Randy like me?" Terry answered quite plainly: "Jealousy." Randy exhibited all the psychological definitions of "middle-child syndrome." He felt overshadowed by Terry, who was confident and self-assured; then when I came along, he felt as if he had been replaced as the baby and forgotten. Of course all that was bullshit because our wonderful parents loved each of us the same, and none of us were ever left out or mistreated.

Whatever the reason, Randy was withdrawn into himself.

As a child, I actually thought he was really cool, and I wanted him to love me so badly. Like, not love me because he felt he had to but because he really did.

He was handsome, with long wavy hair and hip-hugging bellbottoms, barefoot and bare chested. He was the epitome of the '60s hippie.

Sadly, there aren't a lot of standout memories to reminisce about. No hugs. No outward affection. At times he was downright mean to me.

"I hope you broke your back," he snarled to me so our mom couldn't hear. I had taken a really hard fall, and all I wanted, while crying and reaching to him, was consolation and some affection.

Randy told me he loved me only a number of times, and when he did, it only made me feel more sad and bitter toward him. Once I was critically ill and on life support, and in one of my few fleeting moments of consciousness, I heard him say it. It hurt me so deeply because in my reasoning he was only clearing out his own guilty conscience.

Randy and I tried to hang out after we were older, but any comradery was fueled by alcohol and drugs. Eventually you just have to concede and come to the conclusion that it just wasn't meant to be.

Addition: he lost his wife of fifty-one years in 2023 to a rapidly progressively moving form of cancer. At first everything was purposely kept from me, but suddenly I was asked to be a part of the situation. Even after all the animosity between the two of us, I put it all behind me and stepped up to help my brother. We sort of talked about things, and we allowed things to be resolved for the most part. It's not like we have a lot of time to make up for the lifetime we missed, so we will just let things be. I have been taking care of him, providing support as needed to him.

Randy, Linda, Terry

My parents, Mom & Dad

Linda Temple

I Am a Statistic

Molestation

Ninety-five percent of sexually abused children will be abused by someone they know and trust.

Of those molesting a child under six years old, 50 percent are family members.

The most vulnerable age for children to be exposed to sexual assault is between three and eight years old.

My grandfather passed away when I was about three years old. I don't really remember much about him except that he smoked a pipe continually while sitting in his green vinyl recliner in their living area. The smell of the pipe smoke was comforting to me while I sat in his lap. My grandmother, whom I lovingly called Nanie, would always be off in the kitchen, cooking some fabulous meal and skinning fish. Nanie meant everything to me, and besides my mom, I probably learned the second most from her, and she spoiled me rotten. To this day I can still feel the thin, paperlike skin of her hands. Her fingertips were cracked and callused from the years of hard work. Nanie had one fault, and that was her son, James Archie Jr. (aka Bugs). Bugs was a result of his environment because Nanie treated him like a child his whole life. He was a bachelor who never worked a day in his life. In all aspects he was an eternal child playing games, doing crossword puzzles, fishing, building remote-controlled airplanes, and riding bicycles.

He wasn't mentally impaired but rather very intelligent. He was obsessive, and when he became interested in something, he would go in on it all the way. He would speak using every obscenity imaginable. He had an unhealthy obsession with flatulence. You would also need to have nerves of steel to be in a vehicle with him, because he drove like a bat out of hell.

The house always had kids over hanging out with him. Bugs was a grown man, yet no one considered this to be odd or inappropriate. It was always perpetual playtime, and if you didn't let him win at the games, he would throw a temper tantrum, and you were made to go home. I guess I was nearly four years old, and I was sitting on the living room floor with Uncle Bugs, playing some game. I will never forget the crazy grin on his face, the kind of grin children have when they know they have been very bad. My face flushed, and my eyes glazed over as I stared toward my grandfather's empty green vinyl recliner and his portrait on the wall behind it. I was confused as I got up and ran into the kitchen with Nanie. I hid between her and the kitchen cabinet, gripping tightly to her apron. He quickly followed me like an animal hovering to pick away at my flesh. "Leave her alone…" Nanie snarled at him. I was terrified. I hated him. I felt sick. I wanted my mother to come and pick me up.

My mother and father both worked when I was little, and since children's facilities were not really a big thing at the time, I had to stay with Nanie. There just weren't many options for parents.

I was so anxious, so the moment I sat down in the car I told my mother what had happened. I wasn't sure how she would react or if she would even believe me. She took a deep breath, told me to stay in the car, then went back into the house. I was expecting her to be in the house for a long time, but she wasn't, and when she sat down in the car, she seemed almost angry at me. She sternly pointed her finger and said, "You will NEVER mention any of this to your father, nor will you ever speak about this again." The next week I was back at Nanie's house with Uncle Bugs as if nothing had ever happened. I really wasn't the same, and it changed my personality. I grew older, and I was no longer a bubbly, bouncy little girl. Instead I became shy and awkward, especially around men. I didn't want to be touched or patted in any way. It caused me to be fearful of men that I had no reason to be afraid of, friends of my parents who were respectable and would have never hurt me. I personally believe that as I matured into a sexual adult, it was the pivotal reason I became so promiscuous.

It was very well known that many molestation victims at that young age of development are later diagnosed with dissociative identity disorder, which develops to protect their delicate psyches. We know this from cases such as those in the well-known books *Sybil* and *When Rabbit Howls*. This did not occur with me. Instead my memory was buried deep inside my mind.

I was pregnant with my own daughter in 1993. I was happily married to the man of my dreams, and I thought my life was perfectly normal until "it" happened. The memory, for whatever reason, decided it was time to claw its way out from its hiding spot in my mind. Driving down the highway with my husband, I began to cry as piece by piece the memory resurfaced. Doug looked over at me and reacted. "Honey, what's wrong?" The sporadic memories swirled in my mind, making me dizzy as I responded, "I was molested."

I couldn't get home fast enough because I wanted to call and ask my mother, "Did this happen?"

You could tell she felt almost trapped, knowing she had to give me a reason why something like this was allowed to happen. "Yes, it did." She didn't have much to say except "Sometimes, in certain families, things like this just happen." At that particular point in time, that was all I could hear and comprehend. Years later we were able to talk about it in more detail, and she confided in me about the issues of incest within her family. She had been sexually assaulted by her father as well as her brother Bugs. We talked about a lot, and I was happy that everything had been talked about in detail, not shoved under the carpet. I knew how painful this topic was for my mother, and I also knew we would never speak of it again. Throughout the many years to come, more information was made available to me by the many cousins and multiple neighbors who came forward to me. My uncle Bugs was never brought to justice but beaten up by neighbors, ostracized by his remaining family, and left to rot in a mentally crazed solitude.

I sought counseling. I wanted answers and to try and understand. How much more was buried deep inside me? Would my mind protect me and keep it buried away? I got a lot of answers. I learned that a memory such as this is extremely rare to recover. I heard that scary word "dissociative" and that it was the reason why a memory that has been forgotten is then years later recalled. My counselor taught me how to deal with the memories, and I got a lot of answers, but that was about it. It was up to me and in my process to get through the anger and find forgiveness. To be honest, everyone needs to know this isn't something new; this happens within families in the past and the present and will continue in the future. This is an illness and a learned behavior. Education is the key! My uncle Bugs was also a victim of incest, but the window for getting help had long passed him up. After the death of his beloved dog, after years of solitude and a mind engulfed in schizophrenia, he sat down in my grandfather's green vinyl recliner and blew his brains out with a shotgun.

I didn't cry.

Please educate your children about body safety in the earliest of years. Empower them because it might well be the difference between a child becoming a statistic or not.

Reading, Writing, and Arithmetic

All Learned to the Tune of a Hickory Stick...

Yeah, I went to school when math was actually called arithmetic and all the subjects were taught in one room. It is unknown how the hierarchy among children takes place, deciding who will be popular or not, but I think it happens in the early stages of school, and teachers are in on it. I wasn't one of the lucky kids, and I really don't know why. My mom dressed me nice, and I was always well groomed. I was painfully shy and awkward, so I am sure that might have been my downfall. I was more awkward and unpopular than this kid named George. George was a kid that would randomly vomit without any reason at all. It never failed because it happened every day—you just learned not to stand too close to George. I often wondered what ever happened to George. I didn't have a lot of friends, and most of the kids were cruel. This one girl named Lenora would try to pinch my butt cheeks with her shoes on the back of the desk seat. Once she managed to pinch the fuck out of my ass. Oh man, it hurt so badly, and I went crying to my teacher, who really didn't give one shit as she pulled me to the hallway. She told me to settle myself down because I was disrupting the class.

I went to school when the principal carried a long wooden paddle and it was all right for the principal to use it on you. In my elementary school, the principal was a tall, heavyset woman named Mrs. Henry. She would walk up and down the hallway, methodically patting that wooden paddle repeatedly in the palm of her hand, creating an air of intimidation. I only had one run-in with Mrs. Henry. I had to go to the bathroom, so I got permission from my teacher and left the classroom. I walked on the left side of the hallway with my hands held behind my back, because that's how it was done back then. I got to the bathroom just as a class was taking its break, and of course a few of the girls started pushing me around, not letting me in the stall to do my business. My teacher notified the principal that I had been gone too long, so guess who was waiting outside the bathroom for me? You guessed it! Mrs. Henry. She grabbed my arm, led me to her office, and sat me down. She accused me of playing around in the bathroom.

"No! I was not!" Tearing up, I muttered, "I was pooping." She wasn't amused and threatened to paddle me—that is, until I broke down crying. Instead of getting a paddling, I was let off with a warning. I dried my tears and walked back to class, and as I entered the room, I cut my eyes toward my teacher. "Traitor," I thought to myself.

Recess was pure hell! Choosing teammates was a cruel form of torture for a young psyche. George, the vomiter, was chosen for a team before I was. I am scared and still suffer from Vietnam-like flashbacks from the dreaded dodgeball. The object of the game is to eliminate all the members of the opposing team by hitting them with the thrown balls. Dodgeball basically made it legal for all the big, strong kids to completely beat the shit out of the weak and meek kids. The coach would walk to the center of the court while pulling a large rolling basket carrying approximately thirty large rubber balls. With his foot perched on top of the basket, he was Moses parting the Red Sea, bellowing out, "FIGHT!" He would kick the basket of balls over. For the next thirty minutes or so, it was like Normandy. Balls taking kids' legs out from under them, balls bouncing off their heads, rapid fire taking out two or three kids at a time. Some kids tried their best to fight back, but most didn't have a snowball's chance in hell. I figured my best way to survive was to drop, roll into a ball, then try to protect my head.

School was similar to prison. You must seek out protection if you wish to survive. The best way to protect yourself from being beaten up was to befriend a bigger kid or a mean kid. I actually never got beaten up, thank goodness, just overlooked and ignored.

My grades were decent in elementary school, but as I matured, it was very evident that I wasn't the sharpest crayon in the box. I tried hard, though. Mom and Dad never punished me. Instead they would say, "Just try your very best, baby."

In fifth grade, God decided I wasn't peculiar enough yet and that I would complete my grade school years with a pair of gold-rimmed wire octagonal glasses. It wasn't cool to wear glasses back then; it was a curse. "Check out Four-Eyes!"

Things couldn't get much worse, or could they?

It Doesn't Get Much Better—Middle School

Grades Six through Eight

Entering middle school was really scary! Till this point, all our subjects were taught from one classroom, and now we had a schedule with a different teacher and classroom for each subject. We were just little kids! How did they expect us to handle all this?

Middle school was a large, two-story building, not anything like our little elementary school. No more rules like having to walk on the left side of the hallway with our hands held behind our backs. After the new routine became familiar to us, we all had a sudden realization that we were growing up. I was beginning to grow up too. I had a small group of friends, and we had loads of fun together cutting up. I belonged to a clique. A misfit clique, but a clique nonetheless. I struggled with grades and studying, so any activities away from school were welcomed. We would have slumber parties at one another's houses, and they had nothing to do with sleeping. We would do everything we could to stay awake. Once we were staying at a friend named Donna's house. She lived on one of the busiest streets, so what better idea than to go running right down the center of the street with cars rushing by. It was exhilarating, and for the first time, I felt so free and so wild. We had no idea how the memories of that night would impact us for the rest of our lives. Three weeks later we were all arriving at school, and we all realized Donna wasn't there. We settled into homeroom class to do attendance and listen to the morning announcements. The principal spoke in a solemn tone as he explained the tragic death of Donna. I can't remember any of what he said because I was literally in shock. Basically she left her house, walking down the busy street toward the store, and on her way back home she was struck by a car and killed. Three weeks earlier we were doing the very same thing.

The bottom was about to fall out again. My parents had been noticing something odd about my back, so they immediately took me to the doctor. I was diagnosed with scoliosis, curvature of the spine. The doctors assured my parents that this was a moderate case and probably wouldn't progress any further if they would have me fitted into a body brace that I would end up wearing for several years. The body brace itself was not painful, but the stigma of having to wear it through some of the most formable years was. My closest friends were supportive and protective of me, but there was still a certain amount of ridicule. And with all that, the book closed on my middle school years. I was left with the hope the summertime would lift me up and my outlook would improve. Let's just say I was going to get a visit from dear Aunt Flo—yeah, my period. My morning began with a subtle yet persistent cramp in my abdomen. I headed to the bathroom, pulled down my panties. My heart sank. "BLOOD?" I screamed out.

My mother opened the door to see me sitting there on the toilet crying. She halfheartedly smiled, and with her hands clasped together, and in a gentle voice, she said, "It's a miracle, honey." I was born at a time where you just didn't talk about things, so that was really all that was said. Instead I was handed this small paper booklet, the kind you can get at the doctor's office, labeled "How to talk to your kids about…" The book was old, and the pages were frayed, and the title stated *Know Your Changing Body.* After a few minutes passed, she came back in, and she was carrying some kind of elastic garter belt contraption with a stuffed pad-like object that was about two feet long. She explained that this was what women had to wear while we were on our periods, but I don't really remember anything else. My mind went numb, and all I could hear was the cartoon voices of mothers. "Wa, wa, wa, you are gonna bleed…wa, wa, wa…for the next…wa, wa, wa…fifty years…" If any form of social life wasn't already dead, it sure as hell was now.

High School

Grades Ten through Twelve

Upon entering high school, you quickly become aware that you were now labeled "freshman fish." There weren't any malicious hazing rituals except for constant teasing by the older students. We all seemed so little compared to everyone else. They were adults and it was very intimidating. Freshman year there was a stabbing, and I remember all the blood in the hallway. I knew the girl who did the stabbing, but she disappeared after that, probably to juvenile detention.

The classes were hard, and I would do just about anything to go home. I would call my nanie (my grandmother) since my mom was working. She would always come get me. We'd usually go fishing and be back before Mom would get off work. We'd sing silly songs such as "Three Little Fishes": "Boop boop dittem dattem wattem chu, and they swam and they swam right over the dam." That was great! Freshman year was all about survival and really the last year of our childhood. From here on out, you had to start maturing, settling in, finding your place. Our school was very cliquish. You were either someone of importance or you weren't. I now belonged to a group of misfits, and we were called the stoners. In all reality, we knew we were really the cool kids and didn't have to be a part of all of those other cliques. At the end of sophomore year and the beginning of junior year, I made the decision to try and come out of my shell, to try harder with my studies, and to try to be a part of the school. I joined some clubs. I joined the school band's flag guard. I was enjoying myself until everything changed for me. The body brace that had become a part of my identity was no longer preventing my scoliosis from progressing. What had started off as a twenty-eight-degree curvature of my spine was now a whopping sixty-three degrees and seriously impeding my everyday activities. It became urgent that I partake in corrective back surgery because the doctor stated if I didn't I would be dependent on a wheelchair. I was terrified. I didn't know if I would survive, much less be able to walk again. School and all my friends would be a thing of the past, and I didn't know if I would ever get to go back and finish. I knew any chance of graduating with my senior class would not happen, but all those minuscule worries wouldn't mean anything compared to what my life would be thrust into.

The back surgery took place, and everything seemed fine until two days later fluids began to fill up every cavity of my lungs to the point where I could no longer breathe. I was placed on a machine that took breaths for me, sighed for me, and provided oxygen to keep my heart beating and my brain alive. My body lay immobile in suspended animation for three months of my life. I never knew just how close to death I really was. In times of consciousness, I would stare at a piece of redwood with a figure of Jesus Christ on a silver cross. Was I already dead? Was I in heaven? In other moments I would scribble almost illegible notes on tiny pieces of paper. Mom kept them all in a box at the bottom of her closet. I just figured in my mind that it had all gone wrong and this lifeless piece of flesh was all that was left of Linda Temple until Easter morning.

As I fell in and out of consciousness, all the tubes were removed, and I took my first unassisted breath. The first thing I focused on was that little piece of redwood with Jesus Christ on the silver cross. You can say or think whatever you want about that day, but at that very moment, I knew I was given another chance at life. I knew that I had a purpose, and I wasn't going to fuck it up. Months of rehabilitation were ahead of me, and I would be in a full-body cast for a full nine months. I was a trouper, blasting through all of it with a whole new take on life. I felt confident in myself, and I held my head high, marching forward.

I went back to finish high school. I was a brand-new person. I wore contact lenses, bleached my hair blond, and wore makeup. I made a whole bunch of new friends. I started participating in school activities. I even had a couple of boyfriends. My senior year I worked through a work-sponsored program. I may not have graduated with my original class, but baby, I did it! I graduated!

Stina

Aerosmith
December 2, 1978

I was helping my mother clean out the back closet. She kept most of her craft items and family keepsakes stored there. Fumbling around, I spied something of interest, something that just didn't quite fit in with the rest of the items. I slowly opened the box while Mom wasn't looking, and my mouth fell agape in disbelief. It was a box of letters from Iceland. The letters were addressed to me, and each one had been opened. Tears filled my eyes as I closed the box and pushed it back into its spot.

The only thing I really cared about at twelve years old was this musical group from Scotland called the Bay City Rollers. Oh my goodness, they were so adorable dressed in their short pants and all that Scottish plaid. I was the epitome of a teeny-bopper with a capital *T*. My mother fed my desire by buying all the teen magazines, such as *Tiger Beat* and *Sweet Sixteen*. To say my brothers were disappointed in my musical tastes was an understatement. I didn't really have any close friends growing up, or at least none that shared the same interests as me. I was very lonely and yearned for companionship. Would I ever meet someone that shared the same interests as me? Enter into the picture my third cousin Kristin. I can't be 100 percent sure how we met, but I believe it had something to do with our grandmothers, who incidentally were sisters. We met at her grandmother's lake house. This home was amazing! It was so huge. It had a boat and dock too. The moment Kristin and I met, an almost immediate connection was made. She was the most beautiful girl I had ever seen—amazing blond hair and blue eyes. Kristin's father was my second cousin, and he had married a breathtakingly beautiful Icelandic woman, which made Kristin half Icelandic. Kristin also loved all the same things as me, including the Bay City Rollers.

Our dreams of meeting the Bay City Rollers came crashing down when they canceled all their US tour dates. We were devastated. How could we ever rise from the ruins and carry on? Such drama, right? It wasn't long before our interests turned to a "real" rock and roll band called Aerosmith. I'm not really sure how that transition occurred, going from the Bay City Rollers to Aerosmith, but from those ruins of our heartbreak, we were more mature. Aerosmith was older, nitty-gritty, and mysterious. We were hooked, and our obsession would take us places we could never have imagined.

Kristin and I conspired to spend as much time as we could together. We never grew bored of each other. Our days were filled with so much fun laughing, putting on pretend concerts where we were the band, and daydreaming. We wrote fantasy stories where we would marry Steven Tyler and Joe Perry from Aerosmith. Of course it didn't matter that they were already married; that wasn't going to muck up our plans because Steven and Joe would meet us, and they would fall in love. I really can't remember whose idea it was or if it was a mutual idea, but we took our fantasy stories to the next level by acting out our fantasies for Steven and Joe. She would be Joe for me, and I would be Steven for her. This was purely innocent in the fact that we were not physical with each other. I think we both knew that it could be considered inappropriate if anyone else knew, so we decided to keep a secret and only play pretend when we were totally alone. I think that was another reason we loved the lake house so much—because it provided us the privacy we wanted.

December 3, 1979, was the night all our dreams would come into fruition. In our hands we held two floor concert tickets for the Aerosmith concert right in our very own town. We were dressed in identical satin outfits, and we were ready. The lights inside the Tarrant County Convention Center flashed off and on. The crowd began to scream and push toward the stage. Kristin and I weaved through all the people until we found ourselves standing right against the stage. The lights dimmed for what seemed like forever. Then suddenly the lights flashed back on, and the band was in front of us, blasting out its music. We were screaming like crazy! It felt like they were only performing for us, so Kristin and I put on our little show performing for them, flirting and dancing. Steven would hold his scarf-draped microphone down in front of us, urging us to sing along. Joe knelt down, holding his guitar in front of us to strum. Kristin and I were ecstatic. We were part of this moment, the band, the music, and all those people. But... suddenly it all stopped, and the show was over. My mother, who had accompanied us to the show, had been talking to a

Fort Worth police officer who was there for security. He had special access backstage, so he escorted us back to try and meet the band. We met the bassist, Tom Hamilton, first, and he laughed with us that his handwriting resembled Egyptian hieroglyphics. Joe Perry was very mysterious as he pointed at us through the darkened limousine windows. The backstage area began to clear out, but we realized that we hadn't yet met Steven Tyler. How could he have slipped by us without even a glimpse? "He hasn't come out yet!" someone yelled out. We hurried over, pushing ourselves close to the doorway. Then we saw him strolling down the hallway until he was finally standing in front of us. He tossed an orange from one hand to the other, then slid his hand to my cheek. He gently pulled me toward him and kissed me on the lips. I didn't want the moment to end, but then he repeated the same action with my cousin Kristin. Let me explain something to you...People go through their whole lives never experiencing a dream come true, and there I was...thirteen years old, receiving my very first kiss from the rock god himself, Steven Tyler.

Kristin and I were completely unaware that our life together was ominously on borrowed time. We never thought anyone could ever separate us, but we were wrong. Through peering eyes, whispers, and suspicion it was conceived that our togetherness was becoming an unhealthy situation. My parents were the conspirators who had convinced everyone our relationship was inappropriate. I was only thirteen years old and very naive. What did they think was really going on? Incest? That we were lesbians? Number one, I sure as hell didn't know what that word meant. Number two, I don't even think that was a word back then. Kristin and I both knew we weren't doing anything wrong; it was all perfectly innocent. Why were we being made to feel so ashamed? No one talked to me about it. No one explained anything to me. What had they told Kristin? Did she just not love me anymore? They had even banned us from talking to each other. My heart was broken. I loved Kristin, and they took her away from me. Kristin and her mother moved back to Iceland. I was left alone and confused. I wrote letters but finally stopped because Mom complained about the expensive postage charges.

Years later, after my mother had passed away, we were cleaning out the house. I went to the back room to claim that box of letters, but to my disdain the box and all its contents were gone.

"You Two Are So Happening..."

My Best Friend, Debbie

How do I write everything I want to say about one of the single most important persons of my life, a person whom I have known for forty-six years and who undoubtedly knows me better than I know myself? Debbie is my female hetero life partner, and we were truly destined to be together because we had a special kind of magic to make all our dreams come true. Has it always been perfect? Hell no! Debbie and I could fight harder than anyone I knew, and we sometimes wouldn't speak for years at a time. The thing about Debbie and me was you couldn't keep the type of force we shared apart from each other. It would have been an unnatural thing to do.

I had female friends when I was younger, but I didn't have that one special person that I shared my hopes and dreams with. I met my cousin Kristin, but as close as she and I were, I doubted that the force to make our dreams come true was there. We never had that chance to discover what our future would become, because our parents separated us from each other. However, in her infinite knowledge and love for me, Kristin would not leave me alone. I received a letter from Iceland a few weeks after her move, and I couldn't contain my excitement as I hurriedly read through it, and at the end of the letter she told me all about a girl she knew in school before she moved to Iceland. She explained that she just knew that we would get along really well and I should definitely give her a call. I was very nervous to call her out of the blue; what if she didn't like me? Needless to say I put my little bravery hat on and placed the call. Without our even seeing each other, it was an immediate connection. I can't remember everything we talked about or even how long we stayed on the telephone, but we couldn't wait to meet each other over the weekend. Honestly I think her mother may have been more protective of her than my mother was of me, so the decision was made that I would spend the night with her. I knocked nervously on the front door, hearing a large barking dog. I stepped back a bit as the door opened to reveal the most beautiful girl I had ever seen. Immediately I imagined there was no way that she would want to hang out with a homely-looking girl like me. "Come on in!" She led me directly to her bedroom, and my eyes widened with joy upon seeing the gigantic KISS superposters on her ceiling as well as all over her walls, rock magazines strewn around, and her stereo with albums. I felt a wave of relief rush over me, and I suddenly became aware that everything was going to be absolutely perfect. We were like two pieces of a puzzle that fit together and had been lost until then. We talked about the stupidest things and laughed for hours and hours. She showed me how to "hot box" our music by getting into the closet together, pulling the stereo speakers in, and blasting out the music as loud as we could so we could experience every single breath the rock stars would take. I don't think we slept one wink that whole night because neither of us wanted it to end.

Debbie & Linda

It didn't take long for us to realize that we had found our equals, and we wanted to spend every second we could together, and even then it wasn't enough. We were on the telephone continually, probably driving our parents absolutely crazy. That was way before call waiting or any sort of thing like that. I remember times we would talk so long that one of us would fall asleep. We started writing fantasy stories about our favorite rock stars having sex with us and even marrying us. We knew my mother was famous for policing my stuff when I wasn't around, so we decided to be very clandestine, creating codes for different things such as having sex with rock stars. Oh my God! My mother and Debbie's mom too would have lost their ever-loving minds reading about how much sex we were having in our fantasy stories. So we decided our code for "having sex" would be replacing those words with "around the corner." It was brilliant! Debbie would take our fantasy story notebook one whole week so she could write in it, even at school, hoping not to get caught; then I would do the same the next week. Believe it or not, I kept all those fantasy notebooks for so many years, stacks and stacks. I thought we were so ahead of our time, writing all our dreams down like that, until years later I found out about fan fiction being all the rage and how it is basically taking over the internet. When Debbie would stay at my house, we would put on pretend concerts with a hairbrush as the microphone and a tennis racket as a guitar. We would blurt out Heart's "Barracuda" loudly, thrashing all about just like Ann and Nancy Wilson. Geez! They were so great! I remember one night we were thrashing about in "midconcert" when I swung around with the tennis racket, going into my guitar solo, and I hit Debbie directly in the face. It hurt her, but we fell onto the floor in a complete fit of laughter, and our stomachs hurt so bad from all the laughter. My parents' bedroom was right next to mine, so I don't know how they slept through the madness and never interrupted us at all. They must have thought we were absolutely insane.

We'd get out of the house and wreak havoc too. My parents would take us to the mall every day or so, with our pockets full of money, and leave us there for the whole day. This was back in the '70s, and the mall was the coolest place to hang out. They had an arcade game place called Space Port, and we would go in there, putting quarter after quarter into the machines. We would go get pizza at the Italian pizza parlor and sit there flirting with the full-blood Italian hunks for hours. We were sure they were in love only with us. Haha! We would lie on the floor at the bookstore reading rock magazines for hours until the clerk would eventually chase us off. Don't even get me started about how cool the record stores were back then, and that is where we would spend most of our time and of course would spend most of our money.

During this period of time, this new trend of air guitar became really popular, and everyone was doing it. Basically you would get up on a stage and pretend like you were a band, had an imaginary guitar, the whole thing. It was as much fun as it was ridiculous. This local radio station had put together an air guitar contest event at this local rock and roll bar in Fort Worth, Texas, called I Gotcha, and Debbie and I decided that we were gonna do it. Of course we were underage, so we had to sign up with a chaperone to get into the bar. But wouldn't you know it—when it came down to the day, Debbie's mom decided that she wasn't allowed to do it. So there I was on my own, and I threw caution to the wind and decided to go for it. There is something that you need to know—I had had major back surgery, and I had a complete body cast from my hips to just under my arms, so it sort of wasn't a typical situation. I planned the whole thing out. I was a huge fan of Judas Priest and decided I would do my performance to the Judas Priest song "Diamonds and Rust." The lead singer would usually ride a giant Harley-Davidson onstage, so I decided I would ride a tricycle. And finally as a mic I was going to use a rubber shark. I can't believe that I did it, but I did. Everyone went mad, screaming and clapping. I came in second place, but it was just the experience that made it all worth it. Debbie said she was listening on the radio and they actually talked about me. They said there was this chick who was singing into a rubber shark and how awesome it was.

If our favorite bands were touring, we would go to their concerts too. Debbie was dating Sonny during this period of time, and we called that the "stoner days" because the coolest thing to do was get the tickets up on the balcony so we could smoke all the marijuana we wanted without getting caught. Remembering those concerts is a little fuzzy, but probably the best concert I ever saw during that time was Queen.

The local museum had a planetarium, and at midnight it would have a laser light show with all our favorite music blasting through the speaker system. We would smoke tons of marijuana till midnight, getting completely obliterated before we went because it made the whole experience so much cooler.

Going to concerts lit the flame under us and left us only wanting more. Grounds were rumbling because changes were definitely on the horizon, and if there were any two people that could make their dreams happen, it was Debbie and I. We made magic happen. Debbie and Sonny even transferred to my high school so that we could graduate together. We also started our magazine *On the Road* together with Sonny and with my good friend Sheila "Release the Nip" as our photographer. *On the Road* was the catalyst for us to get closer to the bands and gain access to the backstage areas. Debbie and I both were aspiring writers, and having our very own magazine was another dream come true. It also made us stand out professionally from any of the other girls, along with getting us unlimited access to our local band scene. We finally got our big break when we were able to spend time with Ozzy Osbourne's band. We also managed to add Quiet Riot, Mötley Crüe, Axe, and Twisted Sister to our accreditations. Sadly all the many hours of hard work fell through due to the excessive printing costs, and although we were heartbroken, we knew we had to go on. Summer of 1984, Debbie and I were ready to try and make our way out into the great big world, and of course we would do all this together. How else? Debbie once wrote, "The backstage file doesn't even scratch the surface of all the shows we saw during this period in our lives. We were really lucky because we were being 'scene queens' back when bands had huge budgets for touring and promoters actually sought pretty girls to just make the backstage look better. There was tons of booze, food, restaurants and drugs too."

ON THE ROAD
Newsletter-Magazine
'your metal'

Sonny, Release the Nip Sheila, Linda, & Debbie

The apartment we shared with our mutual friend Lenise was everything we had dreamed it would be, and everyone wanted to be a part of our lives, our wild and crazy ride. I try to put it into words over and over that there was something absolutely magical about the energy Debbie and I possessed. It seemed we were always in the right spot at the right time for something amazing or unusual to happen, and we even laughed at it too. If you ask me, I believe that this sort of magic happens only once in a lifetime. If you are lucky, you get to experience it, and Debbie and I were the lucky ones. The dream couldn't last forever, and eventually time would inevitably take its toll on us. We were living fast and hard, and the cliché of burning the candle at both ends was an understatement. It had really begun to take the biggest toll on me, and I decided to move home. Drugs had ravaged my health. Debbie and I had already begun to drift apart because we were both maturing and wanting different things from our lives. We knew we would always be there for each another and loved each other deeper than anyone could. Life would take Debbie to New York City for a world of big business, travel, and death metal. Life would lead me to the love of my life, marriage, and motherhood. We were living completely different lives, sometimes almost a world apart, but even then our hearts beat in unison. Before Facebook, our snail mail always found its way to each other—with photographs, of course, so we could live through each other's experiences.

Debbie once wrote, "It seems my life began in 1977 when I met Linda."

Debbie was everything to me, and from the moment I first laid eyes on her, I knew my life would never be the same. My God! She was absolutely beautiful, incredibly smart, and funny. She made me want to be a better person. She made me believe that I actually could be whatever I wanted to be.

I copied Debbie: "It seems MY life began in 1977 when I met Debbie."

Debbie, I loved you then, I love you now, and I will love you as I draw my last breath. Thank you for allowing me to be a part of your magical life all these years. See you on the other side, sister.

"Are you sisters?"

"You're not from Texas, are you?"

"The two of you are so different from all the other girls."

"Oh, I love your hair."

"You two are so happening."

Changes

7/23/1984

Lapses of time and memories run deep
Others only wish they could know this life too
Working so hard to have it come so easy
Meticulous planning that never goes awry
Receiving glories hard earned and deserved
It's a power trip that cannot be equaled
The waves of attention
The rush of adrenaline
It serves as a catalyst
To drive us harder
We know the ways of
And to the stars
Astronomically speaking (of course)
Sitting on the very edge of the universe
Primping and posing
Trying not to fall off

Eddie Van Halen & David Lee Roth

"Horse, You Are So Funny!"

Van Halen

November 25, 1980 —
Autograph-signing party in Dallas, Texas
July 15, 1984 — Reunion Arena

The beginning of the '80s would bring about one of the largest party bands that have ever existed. The parties would be taken to all-new levels of depravity and excessiveness. Two little boys from the Netherlands with a very unique last name would go on to influence the future of all rock and roll, including every up-and-coming musician for the next twenty to thirty years. The band was Van Halen.

I was too young to attend the actual concert in Dallas, Texas, where they were the opening act for Black Sabbath. I was, however, lucky enough to catch them at an autograph-signing party at Peaches Records and Tapes on November 25, 1980. It was literally mass hysteria! What better introduction than to parade those luscious lads around in front of every girl that could be squeezed into that record store? The cash was flowing on CDs and posters. I was pretty small, and it felt as if I were being crowd-surfed up to the front, where I was able to get autographs and my first in-person view of the guys. There was no turning back now. This is going to be good, I thought to myself.

By the time the band had finished its first introduction tour, the musicians would be able to set out on their own. Anyone and everyone was trying to grab ahold of something just to be on what was to become one hell of a wild fuckin' ride. Guess who was going to have front-row seats and VIP backstage passes? You guessed it! Lenise, Debbie, and me. We acquired our backstage passes from one of our close friends, the promoter of the show. If we didn't know we had to be a part of this momentous event, he certainly did. On July 15, 1984, Reunion Arena would come to a complete eruption of energy.

Well, I can't say that any of us remember much of the concert itself, because the three of us (along with a cluster of other females) had been herded together into a large dressing room backstage. We were all confused at why we were being held against our will while the roar of the music reverberated throughout the walls of the arena. Suddenly our wonderment was interrupted by a beautifully blond, vibrant, and magnetic woman with an entourage of assistants carrying a couple of boxes full of traditional Mexican dresses. It was Fleur Thiemeyer, famous costume designer for numerous world-renowned rock stars. She just happened to have David Lee Roth, the lead singer of Van Halen, as a client, but tonight she would be our clothing designer. The concert was just one facet of the big show—the second half would be a huge Mexican fiesta celebration when the concert was completed. The girls, including us, were to be the main course. Fleur held in her hands a pair of scissors and a measuring tape, and from her hands she created Mexican dresses for us all to wear...very short, very ripped up and torn, and some that were just pieces tied around us. The Mexican food was plentiful! The drinks were endless! The scantily clad women being the highlight. Well, that and the many bowls of M&Ms—without the brown ones, of course. I remember talking to the band members throughout the night and also all the other very interesting people that we had the pleasure of meeting. The night slowly dwindled down as the band members left for their hotels. Most paired up, but I remember just being tired and just not terribly interested in any hookups that were in the works. I just wanted to head back to our apartment and bask in the phenomenal memory of the entire night.

Lenise & Linda

Classic Girl

Lenise

Mysterious eyes. Sultry lips. Magic bolts of lightning streaming from her fingertips. Rock and roll girl. Affected everyone she touched. Incredibly gorgeous yet so humble she would never think of herself in that way.

While I wrote this book, I had to hold Lenise's chapter till the very end because I knew it would be my hardest to write, and when I did start writing, my eyes filled with tears, and my tears fell to the pages, smearing the ink. I had to get up and go outside for some fresh air as I continued to cry. I honestly think of her every day. There will never be another Lenise. And I am so thankful that I was able to have that beautiful creature in my life.

Debbie and I met Lenise at Ridgmar Mall. We instantly knew she had to be a part of our group, so she took the chance to move out with us. It was like the perfect constellation of stars coming together.

I have weaved stories of Lenise throughout this book because none of the stories could be told without her presence. But don't worry. I have saved a few little stories for this chapter.

Lenise and I could always have fun when we were together—mischievous fun sometimes, but fun all the same. One time we were up to no good, running around Dallas and undoubtedly getting overly intoxicated. Nothing from that day or what we were doing comes to mind, but it is the drive home that night that sticks in my mind. We were in my infamous little Dodge Colt, cruising down a stretch of highway here in Texas called I-30. Okay, so this is where I have to write something so you can visualize what I'm talking about. I-30 was a very dark highway. Lights were on only at exits and in small towns. It had steel railings on the sides to prevent cars from running off the highway. On these long stretches of highway, in between exits, were very steep hills, and there were either marshy, swamp-like areas or in other areas a lake. Lenise kept saying more and more urgently that she had to pee until she finally told me she was going to pee in my car. Nope! No way! I quickly pulled over, and Lenise got out of the car, but there wasn't any room for her to pop a squat between the car and the railing. I need to add that Lenise was blind as a bat, and if she didn't have her contacts or glasses with her, she couldn't see her hand in front of her face. She unbuttoned her pants, stepping over the railing. There was no turning back now, because she literally had no idea where she was stepping. I heard a noise and quickly glanced over. She was gone! I couldn't see her anywhere! I leaned over the passenger seat and in my drunken babble yelled, "LENISE!!! ARE YOU OKAY?"

I heard a faint voice answer back, "Yeah!"

It took a few minutes for Lenise to literally claw her way back up the steep hill, and when she finally made it, I asked her, "Did you pee?" She maneuvered over the railing with her pants still down around her ankles, struggling to pull them up. I tried not to laugh all the way home, but it wasn't easy.

She looked like a mess, grass everywhere. Later that night she told me she spent thirty minutes picking grass out from every orifice.

Lenise always gave the most meaningful gifts, putting a lot of thought into everything. She knew about my love of writing, so for one Christmas she bought me a beautiful leather portfolio equipped with pen and paper, and I still have it today. And one time she went to Hawaii with her family, and when she returned, she had brought me a gold necklace with a dragon emblem, and she told me a dragon was magical and strong like me.

Lenise chose me as her maid of honor when she married Rick. She was the most beautiful bride I had ever seen. I, in turn, also chose her as my matron of honor. She was fulfilling her duties by holding up my wedding dress while I peed, and she looked up into my eyes and said, "You sure you wanna go through with this? We can get you out of here."

Lenise was the first of us to have a baby, beautiful Rachel. I was the first person at the hospital after she had Rachel. She quickly handed her to me and said, "I gotta go smoke." I stood there rocking that beautiful little girl in my arms, and I talked to her about just how very special her mommy was and how lucky she was to have her.

A friend of ours called one night while I was sitting watching television with my daughter. I knew it couldn't be good news, and I was afraid of what she was about to tell me. Lenise had died from an accidental overdose. I screamed uncontrollably, "NO!!!" I cried for so long. I was numb. I had just seen her at the Rail Club when they threw a huge birthday party for all the rockers who were turning fifty and who already were fifty. How could we have had so much fun, and now she was gone? How could I not have known that she was taking heavy drugs? I was just lost.

There was no funeral, only a cremation. No farewell? No goodbye? I phoned her ex-husband, Rick, and told him I was planning a memorial for her, and he was all in. So many people came for their farewells, even Rex Rocker from Pantera. Her magic touched so many people, and now we all had to adjust.

* * *

"Did you miss me while you were
looking for yourself out there?"
—"Drops of Jupiter," Train
RIP
Born December 26, 1965
Died December 20, 2015

The Apartment

1984 through 1985

D ebbie and I had parents who were overly protective of us. My parents smothered me so much that I often felt that I would never be able to break free from them. I think maybe they were afraid that if they let me out into the world, something terrible might happen to me. I also considered that they honestly just didn't think I could take care of myself without them.

That winter we worked tirelessly at Ridgmar Mall in Fort Worth. It truly was the "it" place to work. The mall was always the place to hang out, meet guys, and maybe get into mischief. We saved our money, and we conspired every day with our plan of moving out, making sure we didn't leave out any details. Debbie and Lenise worked at a huge department store called Stripling & Cox. I worked as a manager at Parklane Hosiery. Debbie met Lenise while working at Stripling & Cox, and we liked her so much that we asked her to join us, and she agreed. We would meet at the local bookstore on our breaks, fumbling through the pages of as many rock magazines we could get our hands on. We inspected every picture of the New York club scene and all the bands that played at places such as CBGB. We also were very interested in Hollywood Boulevard in California because it was where all the '80s glam bands were originating from. It was so exciting. We knew that there wasn't any way we could move to any of these places because it was way out of our league at that time. We decided the only place that we could move to was Arlington, Texas. It was a huge college party town right in between Dallas and Fort Worth, Texas. We were able to get anywhere fairly easy. It was the perfect place for us all to begin our lives!

Our apartment was a townhome with an upstairs and downstairs, and it was two blocks from the college. Lenise was in college, so this really worked out for her. The bedrooms and full bathroom were upstairs, and the living area, kitchen, and half bath were downstairs. Debbie and I really didn't have anything except our clothing, stereos, album collections and one dresser. We decided that since Lenise had a boyfriend and also most of the furniture, we would let her have the biggest bedroom. Debbie and I were so close anyway—it just made sense for us to share the smaller bedroom. We didn't even have a bed to share, but I did have a flip bed/chair that I slept on. Debbie just threw down some blankets, and she was happy. It was the most cozy apartment, and we really loved it. It was almost like it had its own life experiences while we lived there.

It gave a whole new meaning to the age-old saying "If walls could talk."

The apartment looked normal from the outside and I suppose pretty normal on the inside too, but upon further inspection you would find all the subtle little oddities. For instance, we were constantly going to concerts, so we had an excessive number of backstage passes, along with other music memorabilia, and we started decorating the walls of our downstairs half bathroom with these things. It was very unique and gave all the guests something to look at while doing their business.

I am seriously not sure who started this, but we created what we called our "peter meter," and we had it taped up beside the toilet. Needless to say, I was told by many of our male guests that it made them feel incredibly intimidated. If asked, so many people said they would never forget it.

I remember one day of boredom created mischievousness for Lenise and me to get into.

I don't know why we had several rolls of masking tape, but we looked at each other and started laughing. I am not saying whether alcohol may or may not have been involved, but I lay down with my arms and legs slung about, and Lenise used the masking tape to tape out my body onto the carpet. We thought this was the funniest thing ever, but we did not consider how Debbie would react when she walked into the apartment to see a taped-out, possibly murdered body on the floor. Um, she was briefly upset but quickly figured out that we had been up to no good. We decided for prosperity we would leave the taped body there. Another night of boredom brought about more mischievousness from Lenise and me. The band U2 was in town, and the guitarist's name was "the Edge." Literally, his name was "the Edge." We decided it would be really funny to call the hotels in the area and try to find him. After calling several hotels, we hit it big time.

Me: "Can you tell me if you have a guest there by the name of the Edge?"

Hotel clerk: "First name?"

Me: "The."

Clerk: "And the last name?"

Me, very cautious: "Edge."

Clerk: "One moment."

The phone rang, and I was sure we were being transferred to the police or something, but all of a sudden the phone was picked up, and IT WAS THE EDGE! Lenise and I started squealing and laughing, hanging the phone up. We didn't even talk to him! We were so freaked out that he actually answered the phone.

Times were tight for us, although we never stressed or worried about it. We had to make sure there was enough money put back to pay the rent, but there had to be money to party and go to concerts. Food was the one amenity that we cut corners with. We figured out quickly that if you could buy a large bag of potatoes, you could make a whole lot of meals. Baked potatoes, mashed potatoes, fried potatoes, potato pancakes. The choices were endless. Ramen was our other food of choice. In the '80s it was super cheap, maybe three cents a package, so we ate the shit out of ramen.

My mom would always take pity on us and would bring groceries every once in a while. She would shop at some really cheap surplus store. The labels to *all* the food were white, and the titles were in black lettering. *Everything* was black and white. Trust me, we were very thankful for the food and all the choices, but our cabinets became a laughingstock to all our visitors. We were like, Laugh all you want—at least we are eating.

I had been dating a really great guy by the name of Jeff, and I wanted to impress him with my cooking. I saved enough money to buy a roast, but I suddenly realized I didn't have a pan. We had Asian neighbors that always seemed pretty nice, so I borrowed one of their pans so I could cook Jeff a great meal. Everything went over splendidly, and Jeff was very impressed, and I was happy...until I noticed the pan I had borrowed. It *did* have wooden handles, but after cooking Jeff's roast, I realized the handles were completely burned, cracking, and beginning to fall apart. Oh my God, what was I going to do? I couldn't give it back to them like this. I decided to just go on about our everyday life, ignoring the fact that I had kidnapped their pan indefinitely. One afternoon, a knock came on the door, and I opened it up to see them standing in front of me. In their Asian language, they said, "We want our pan back." I actually don't know what they said, but I am assuming that was probably what they said, along with "You stupid American bitch." I handed them their pan and repeatedly apologized over and over, doing the little bowing action.

I felt so guilty. They gave me a dirty look and left.

We had collected a menagerie of pets, and they fit right in with the craziness of our apartment life. We had a cat, Yngwie, named after a Swedish guitarist. There really wasn't anything unique or different about Yngwie. He just hung out.

We had a dog, Punky, named after another gorgeous guitarist. Punky was awesome, but he was always on the lookout for bigger and better things. One day he just disappeared, and he didn't come back. We were heartbroken. Why would Punky run away from us? We all sat around depressed for a few weeks until one afternoon Punky just came walking in through the sliding doors, walked to his favorite spot, and lay down to rest. He was fucking fat!! He looked happy, though, but he seemed tired. What the hell? We finally figured out that Punky had run away to a Mexican family's home several blocks away. I guess he was just missing us and decided to come home.

We had a parakeet named Elephant Bird. He was named after the Elephant Man, duh! Elephant Bird's beak was all deformed, and he couldn't even talk right because of it. Well, he didn't talk…he squawked. I think because of his affliction he spent most of his time getting high from the secondhand pot smoke that always hung around in our house. He didn't seem to suffer and seemed pretty happy.

One night we were sitting around the apartment, unusually bored. A pounding knock came at the door. We opened it, and there was a silver stretch limousine with a 6'5" chauffeur standing there. A couple of heavy metal friends had rented it for the night just to kill the Sunday boredom, and we left with them for a long night of partying.

I worked a lot of different places while we lived in Arlington. I remember I had a really good job at Stripling & Cox, the department store, and I made pretty good money. I had scheduled time off so I could go to Austin to see KISS and when they played Dallas too. When the day approached and the manager of the entire store told me I couldn't have that day off, I was pissed off. I argued with him that I had already put in for those days off, but he said it didn't matter and I couldn't take it off. Guess what I did? I QUIT! Priorities, dude! Priorities! There was a huge party that night at the apartment.

At one time I worked at a Pizza Inn, and I wouldn't get off until two in the morning. At the end of the night, all the pizzas and food leftovers I took home. So all the clubs would be closing, and all the random partiers would start congregating at our apartment, ready to chow down. The party would sometimes last all night.

Our apartment was centrally located, and we always had people coming to our apartment to hang out and party with us, and we were rarely ever totally alone. Pantera was always coming over to hang out. Rigor Mortis, who were some of our best friends, would always hang out. We had regulars. Our very good friend Donny would come over every Friday night, but he would stop beforehand at Big Daddy's liquor store, pick up whatever liquor was on the Friday night special, then bring it back for us to get obliterated on. One night in particular stands out as being one of the worst drunk moments I have ever had. The liquor that Friday night was 100 percent peppermint schnapps that we mixed with iced tea. There is just a huge cloudy haze. In the morning when I woke up, there was vomit streaming down the wall of our staircase, then all over the living room. I finally found Debbie, and she was wrapped around our downstairs half bathroom's toilet, passed out completely. Donny was gone. I could never drink peppermint schnapps ever. If I even think about it, I am going to start hurling. We asked Donny why he would come over every Friday night just to get us drunk and then leave, and he would just say he loved seeing us have such a good time.

We had another friend named Ricky, and he was one of our favorite people. He would just randomly show up at our apartment, always barefooted. Wherever he would sit down, he would usually go off to sleep for hours. Once, he fell asleep on our staircase. We thought he was so cute that we would cover him and just step around him. It wasn't until many decades later that I would find out from him that he was between twelve to sixteen years old and homeless. If we had known that, we would have taken him in to live with us. Ricky told me once, "I had never been embraced in such an awesome environment as yours."

We had neighbors on one side who were college students. Two dudes who once signed their autographs for me. One's name was Johnny, and I think he may have been a DJ. The other dude's name was Pete, and he was sort of quiet, had a good sense of humor, and was a guitarist. I would sit in my bedroom against the wall in between our bedrooms. He would sit and play acoustic guitar for me, especially when he knew I was feeling homesick and lonely. His guitar playing got me through many hard times, and I will never forget it. We created little knocks back and forth to each other that we understood. Oddly, it never crossed our minds that maybe we should get to know each other and possibly date.

Another neighbor was Mike, and he was a local dealer. He was one of our favorite people, and he had a Doberman pinscher. He even wrote a poem for us once, and I still have it.

Headbangers 1985

The three of you are honest
You live it to the whole
Through times of strife
Both day and night
You like to rock and roll
Headbangers, I call you
Though affection fills my voice
'Cause though you're wild
And never mild
You live a life of choice

Linda, you're the softest
You seem sometimes out of place
But when the volume
Fills the air
A smile lights up your face
Lenise, you are mysterious
You have a mystic look
But who am I
To wonder why
'Cause Alice wrote your book
And now we're down to Debbie
The last but not the least
She lives to eat
All rock and roll
And concerts are her feast.
I wrote this for the three of you
So you would understand
I love you all like sisters
And I should be in a band

Sadly, the day came when the apartment and all the events that happened there would be only a part of everyone's memory. I moved out in late 1985 due to the drug usage and effect it had on me. Lenise and Debbie lived there a bit longer, in a much more of a subdued mood. They decided to throw a huge farewell party and let anyone and everyone show up to pay their respects. We were all there, and so many other people. It was a befitting celebration for a location that brought so much fun and happiness to so many people.

There is an old saying "All good things must come to an end," and I can't think of a better saying that applied to the end of our apartment era. There were really good times, yet there were some bad times too. But there are no regrets, nor would we change anything. Were the objectives of us moving out on our own met? Yes, we took care of ourselves, sort of. We survived. Did we live and do all the things that we had set out to do? I walked out into the parking lot and looked back at our apartment and with a huge smile whispered, "Yeah, we really lived."

Willie Nelson said it perfectly…"Turn out the lights; the party's over."

The only existing photo of The Apartment
Elephant Bird, Body tapped out on floor

The beginning and the end
The best, most memorable
8 months of my life
IT WAS HAPPENING!!

Linda with Jeff Dennis from Eruption

Linda with the infamous MONK

Drugs. Drugs. Gimme Drugs!

1980 through 1990

I grew up knowing that my brothers experimented with drug use, but it wasn't until much later in life that I learned what level of usage they had. Terry had a more level head about him, and he was mainly a connoisseur of marijuana. Randy, however, was known by everyone as "the doctor." I was told that if anyone was searching for a specific type of drug, he would certainly have it in his little medicine bag of goodies.

It was unrealistic to believe that I would never try drugs, but I think for the most part I practiced vigilant behavior. That was one of the pluses of being a third child: I could watch and learn from all their mistakes. First, never let your baby sister see you smoking pot in the driveway because she will fucking tattle on you. I narced on my brothers! I admit it!

I think the first time I ever tried marijuana I was a sophomore in high school. Debbie started dating a really gorgeous dude named Sonny, and he was a massive pot smoker. The three of us were joined at the hip. In fact I bet Debbie and Sonny wished I would have gotten lost sometimes. Sonny introduced us to "the bong" and the dreaded, appalling "bong water."

You spill that shit on your carpet, you might as well burn your house to the ground, because that shit ain't coming out *ever.* You couldn't even try to lie to your mother about the smell; she was young once and knew what that horrific smell was.

One year I had to attend summer school, making up for some classes I had missed. Needless to say, I was pretty bummed out about it. That was until I found out that everyone was stoners. We would get an hour for a lunch period, and we would cram into one car and find somewhere to park. Let the smoking begin! Dude! Summer school was the bomb.

By this time Debbie and I considered ourselves accomplished marijuana users, and we were ready for the big time. What came next? Why not buy our very own first bag of pot? Oh my God, you already know this isn't going to end well. Marijuana was twenty-five dollars for a quarter-pound baggie, and we combined our funds and bought a bag of pot. We were so proud. We went by Sonny's house and bragged, showing him. We got stoned; then Debbie and I decided we wanted to drive over to Arlington to show a guy I was sort of seeing, and it just so happened he was a drug dealer. I didn't find that out until later. We begin our drive, and as we were driving, we were holding the bag up in broad daylight, bragging about how pretty it was and of course how proud we were of each other for our achievement. Okay, I know what you are thinking. Were we stupid, or what? No, we were not stupid, just very naive. It was at that very moment a drug bust was scheduled, and we just happened to be surrounded by all the undercover officers that would have been the ones executing the drug bust. We were sitting ducks, and they decided that these sitting ducks needed to be taught a lesson. Before we knew it, we were completely surrounded by police cars with flashing lights, undercover police cars with flashing lights. We pulled over, frantically fumbling, trying to hide our precious bag of pot. Idiots! They had already seen we had it because we *had* to hold it up and brag about it. What bad luck, right? Yeah, that very moment in time that we were bragging on our pot was the exact moment in time we were surrounded by an undercover drug bust. They made us move to the back of the car, and they proceeded to interrogate us, trying to get us to admit what we were doing. We were too busy crying and pleading for them not to arrest us. They searched my car, and of course they found our precious bag of pot and brought it back, confronting us. We were blubbering idiots, continuing to cry and plead for them please not to call our parents. Wah! Whining babies!

Okay, so I'm sure this whole time they were laughing their asses off, enjoying every second of this ridiculous situation. They could have easily arrested us, but instead they had thought of a much better punishment by making us empty the bag of pot out in the grass on the roadside. We sort of knew at this point that we were not going to be arrested, and we were almost appalled at what they were asking us to do. Pour out our precious bag of pot?? No, we didn't bitch. We fucking dumped that shit out faster than it took us to buy it. It was gone. They said they hoped we had learned our lesson and requested we get in our car and leave. We did, and at first we were very silent, almost in shock at what had happened. We pulled over at a service station and turned to look at each other when we said it. Yeah, we should go back and pick it up off the roadside. Okay, so we didn't do that, but we did seriously consider it. Instead I decided to call the guy I was sort of seeing, who, I remind you, was a drug dealer. I was crying, and he said, "What's wrong?"

In between my crying and huffing, I said, "We got pulled over. There were undercover cops going on a drug bust in Arlington. Can we come over?"

There was one second of silence, and then he yelled out, "DON'T FUCKING COME HERE!!!" Then he hung up. It was years before I lost my fear that I was being followed by undercover cops everywhere I went. Just letting you know, their teaching us a lesson worked…Debbie and I never bought another bag of pot.

The summer of 1984 we moved to the college party town Arlington, Texas, where you could readily get whatever drug you wanted. One out of every ten people would be a drug dealer. Our apartment quickly became party central, and it didn't take long for the local dealers to be alerted to that and the three young women on their own for the first time. Debbie and I began dabbling right away, mostly with cocaine and speed. Lenise, however, was definitely more experienced in the usage of drugs. It was many years until I could really accept just how deeply into drugs she really was too.

We would often leave our downstairs sliding door open, and people we knew—and some we didn't—would randomly wander in just to hang out, bringing us the latest drug to try. There was this one black dude that we didn't know anything about, and he would show up about once a week. He would pull out a bag of cocaine, pour it out onto our glass table, cut out the lines, then call us over to do the snorting. He would nervously peer out the sliding door as if he were being followed or something, and when we finished snorting, he would say goodbye and disappear until the next week. We would just stand there bewildered, confused and high as shit. We had another neighbor who was a dealer, and when we needed something, we would head over to his apartment. He absolutely loved us, and we really loved him too. The night we had to drive to Austin to see KISS, we went by his apartment. He was usually up, and he would just open his refrigerator. He hid his speed in little butter containers, and I can remember fumbling through them, trying to find that little corner tab of speed. There were times we couldn't have done half the things we did without drugs.

The three of us were also going to concerts where we were exposed to countless amounts of drugs, and again all of it was free. We were sitting backstage with a promoter friend of ours, and he poured out a bag of cocaine onto the table in front of us, proceeding to chop it up and spread it out into a large arched rainbow shape. He grinned at us, handing us rolled-up one-hundred-dollar bills, saying, "You girls start on one end and I'll start on the other. Then we'll meet in the middle of the rainbow." Holy shit! We were doing drugs with the promoters, the roadies, the groupies, and of course the rock stars. I remember one time I was doing cocaine with the roadies in one bus, and then the rock star came in and said, "Come with me to our bus—our drugs are better." I got up and went with the rock star to do more drugs. It was ridiculous!

We befriended another girl, and that is when our drug use escalated intensely. Her brother-in-law was *the* cooker/drug dealer in that area, and he would soon be introduced into our lives. One day, once he had gotten to know and trust us, he had gotten word through the grapevine that the cops were possibly looking for him. He showed up at our door, asking to hang out for a bit, and of course we agreed that he could. Then he proceeded to carry in duffel bags full of money, drugs, and weapons. Scary as this sounds, we were completely naïve to the dangers we were in. One night in particular, he showed up at our apartment carrying a briefcase, laid it atop our table, and popped it open to reveal it was completely full of speed. I couldn't believe my eyes. I had never seen that much of a drug in one place before, and not even thinking about the dangers surrounding this event, I just wanted to dive in face first. I made sure Debbie, Lenise and her boyfriend Jeff were all awake and accounted for because I knew they didn't want to miss out on this moment. We were about to get FUCKED UP. You would think that the night would end on a high note right then and there, but no. There was more to come. He left the apartment for about an hour, coming back with a huge nitrous oxide tank. He crafted a mask out of a two-liter bottle so we could breathe in the gas, which we did. You would breathe it in and pass out but then quickly wake right back up. The high that you would experience while you were unconscious was so peaceful that when you woke up you wanted to do it again. I can't remember that night ever ending. My heart hurt. My head was hurting. I was having difficulty breathing. I could not feel my taste buds on my tongue anymore. Jeff and I were hit the worst. I couldn't sleep for days, and even if I could, I didn't want to lie on my bed because he had passed out there and it reeked of ether. I hadn't realized that I could feel that absolutely miserable, but as unbelievable as it sounds, I still wanted more.

By late 1985 I knew I was in trouble. I felt so very sick that it frightened me. I knew that if I didn't stop, I would either be arrested or more likely die because I was so very sick and thin. Debbie and Lenise didn't understand what I was actually going through at this time, and I didn't know how to explain it to them. I kept hearing Vivian Campbell's voice telling me, "This crazy life is not for you. You are better than all this." I knew I had to move home, so I called my brother Terry and simply said, "Please come get me and take me home." Terry and Randy plus some of their friends arrived at my doorstep later that day to take me home. They loaded up my possessions in minutes, and it was suddenly all over. Terry said that he would never forget the amount of drugs randomly strewn all around the apartment, on tables and everywhere, and that he just shook his head in disbelief. Debauchery was the only way that it could be described.

I faced the next chapter in my life, and it would begin with my struggle to wean myself off drugs without any help and without my parents catching wind of what was happening to me.

My parents were generally very naive and trusting people, and I was so afraid they would find out and be so ashamed of me. I don't think I could have taken that at that period. I didn't consider myself an addictive person, but I had let drugs take hold of my mind and my body.

Man, let me tell you that I thought it would be pretty easy for me to just stop using, but I learned really fast that I had a rough and bumpy road ahead of me. The easy availability of drugs created a "foaming at the mouth" drug addict. I would find myself meeting people out at clubs, doing cocaine on the hoods of cars. I would purposely befriend people that I knew had access to drugs just so I could get a fix. I started hanging out with my brother Randy and his wife Sheri, bringing drugs up there to do together. In fact, that period of time might have been the closest I've ever been to him. I honestly cannot tell you the very last time that I did drugs. I can't remember. I realize that it was a very short period in my life, but the amount of drugs that I was able to cram into my body during that time was insane, and what I didn't realize was the amount of damage that it had done to my body. After I was finally clean, I would get violently ill just being around people doing drugs.

I was married in the summer of 1993, and before we could try to get pregnant, I had to have a major sinus surgery to remove polyps and repair the damage to my sinus cavity. This would be the norm throughout the rest of my life; I have had numerous surgeries. I don't know if I am any type of person to give testimonials, but I believe I have a story of survival to tell, and I will tell it to anyone that needs a little help getting out of a bad situation. I have always been open with my children, because believing that they would never try drugs was very unrealistic. It is human nature to try something you know nothing about, but I explained to them that if you do try it, you should have the smarts to decide that it isn't for you and know when to stop. I am very happy to say that my children have never been drug addicts and are very responsible human beings.

I take everything that I have been through as a lesson that has made me the person I am today, and I am proud of who I am today. Drug- and alcohol-free.

Pantera

1982 to 2004
Beginnings and Endings

I was seriously unsure whether or not even to write a chapter on Pantera. There were so many memories, as many bad as there were good. Firsts and lasts. Smiles and laughter. Tears and heartaches. I wrote *my* memories and stories, my truths that *no one* can take away from me.

We were all trying to maneuver through the metamorphosis of adolescence and just trying to hold it all together. Where to begin such an epic story? The very beginning, of course.

Pantera was a band made up of our very own Texas hometown boys. Jerry, their musical entrepreneur father, raised Darrell and Vinnie to be rock stars from day one, teething them with guitar picks and drumsticks. Can you imagine Christmas morning at their house? The living room was probably filled with every bright, shining, chrome, noisemaking musical instrument imaginable. I think it was more up to their wonderful mother, Carolyn, to keep the two of them on track on how to be good human beings and make them complete their education.

The guys in Pantera may have had things come really easy for them in the beginning with the help from their father, but don't think for one minute that they didn't pay their dues, because they did for years. Pantera became a band during a very influential era. During this period it was all about how much of a party band you could be, how much hair spray you used in your hair, and how much spandex you wore on your body. They kept up with the times every step of the way.

Debbie and I first saw Pantera perform in approximately 1982 at Twin Points Lake. They were opening for another local band that had some success and even a local club named after it, Savvy. The guys in Pantera looked so very young, and I couldn't help but shake my head in disbelief because they were phenomenal! The guitarist looked like an impish little boy with a guitar that was half his size, but he handled it amazingly, making sounds come from that guitar that sounded inhuman. It may have been all copy songs, but the bands they were copying owed them a debt of gratitude for making their songs sound so good.

Darrell was about sixteen years old and had already made a name for himself winning numerous contests and guitars. He won his first contest at fourteen years old, when he took home a first-place trophy and a Dean guitar.

All I know is I walked away from the Pantera experience knowing that I had to keep an eye on these guys because mark my words, they were going to be big.

Debbie and I, along with several of our friends, were tirelessly putting together a small street magazine. I actually had correspondents in New York and in California. We followed the metal scene so closely, and we totally believed *On the Road* really had the potential to be something very special. We knew this was the perfect opportunity to interview Pantera and give the guys a feature. It was perfect, because they were a local band working to make a name for themselves, and so were we. So while everyone else worked on writing articles, I worked on getting an interview with Pantera set up. The first attempt was in approximately 1982 at a huge party, heavy meadows in Mansfield, Texas. It wasn't necessarily the perfect location because it was a party and everyone was intoxicated. We conducted the interview in a trailer that was on site, and inside the room was a large Amazon parrot that continued to caw and talk the whole time. Needless to say, it was a bust, and we had to reschedule the interview once again. The second interview was scheduled at an Arlington, Texas, dance club, and after their set was completed, we finally had a completed interview for *On the Road*. They were young, adorable, and crazy boys that definitely needed improvements with their interviewing skills, but of course that was to be expected. I couldn't help but find myself totally hooked, not to mention maybe a little bit enamored with Darrell. He really shined, and I definitely wasn't the only one that saw it.

Over the next year, the changes were rampant. First, our dream of *On the Road* being published came to a complete end. We were heartbroken. The reason was that the price to have it printed was out of our reach. I suppose that from that point on, everyone, including Pantera, looked at us as a joke and thought that we used the *On the Road* magazine to get close to bands. That couldn't have been further from the truth. We had worked hard on something that meant a lot to all of us. Second, Debbie and I moved from both our parents' homes to an apartment in the college party town of Arlington, Texas. Debbie and I both had been so excessively protected throughout our childhoods, so being completely on our own was going to open up an entire Pandora's box for us. Third, we introduced a new friend named Lenise to our little pack, and everything was perfect. Lenise was a mysteriously beautiful girl and added a whole new dynamic to our little groupie coven. Finally, during this period of time I would lose my virginity. Yeah, I was a twenty-one-year-old wannabe groupie queen. My friends would joke that I had hung on way too long. Call me crazy, but I kind of grew up with the concept of being a virgin when I got married, but it was totally unrealistic in this day and time. You just can't be a groupie queen and be a virgin at the same time.

Living in Arlington, Texas, put us right in the middle of Dallas and Fort Worth. Debbie was really unimpressed with Pantera and didn't accompany me, but I tried to see Pantera as often as I could, and since the guys lived in the same area, it made it really easy. I remember hanging out at Darrell and Vinnie's house, which they shared with their mother. On one particular day, I was laying on Darrell's bed, hanging out and talking, when all of a sudden he coughed up a loogie, spitting it onto the wall and then another onto the ceiling. The more grossed out I became, the funnier he thought it was. Carolyn, his mother, was truly the sweetest person, and she put up with so much madness. I remember helping her in the kitchen once, and I asked her how she handled all of it. She sweetly replied, "I just want the boys to have a good time."

The thing about their house was that it was always completely full of hangers-on, people holding on tightly for the wild ride. They had a friend named Dean who always had a lot of money to blow, and he chose to blow most of it on Pantera and all the parties that would constantly be happening around the band.

Pantera was playing an out-of-town gig at the Rock Ranch in Muenster, Texas. This chick we knew decided to rent a limousine because she wanted everyone to be able to get drunk and not have to worry about having to drive anywhere. That chick, me, Lenise, Noelle, Carol, and the legend himself, the Rock and Roll Monk, were along for the ride. Monk was the most famous male groupie—not sexually in any way, but he had met so many famous musicians and had so much memorabilia. Everybody loved him. I loved him! By the time we reached Muenster, Texas, our limousine crew was relatively drunk, and as the Pantera show ended, Darrell and Rex joined for the trip back to that chick's house. It was pretty much chaos with the drinking and smoking marijuana. The limousine driver would buzz in, saying, "Y'all aren't smoking pot back there, are you?"

"No, of course not. We wouldn't do that!" Blowing smoke out the windows.

Once we got back to that chick's house, Darrell told me he was tired and wanted to go home. Even though I was tired too, halfway drunk and not feeling too confident in my driving skills, I drove Darrell home. We sat out in the car talking about all sorts of things, which we did quite often. I always imagined it might have been hard for him to find people to just be able to sit and talk to, but I was always happy to be that person for him. Once I returned to that chick's house, I crashed out sleeping.

We all had so much fun together, and the band continued to climb the ladder of success. It was during this period one of the funniest, most memorable moments happened. There was quite a big group of us gathered together at this Mexican restaurant. There was so much food, there were drinks, and everyone was loud, having such a great time. The restaurant had three Mexican mariachi musicians dressed in traditional clothing, moving from table to table, playing and singing. They slowly made their way to our table. You could tell, as they played their music, that they were trying to impress Pantera and everyone else at the table. Suddenly, they began to perform (with their Mexican accents) the Rolling Stones' "(I Can't Get No) Satisfaction." It was incredible! Darrell was exhilarated and couldn't help standing up and joining in. He even took the guitar from the Mexican guitarist and started playing along with them. It was a monumental moment, and I will never forget it.

The late '80s brought about so many changes it was almost hard to keep up. In late 1985 I made the decision to move back home with my parents.

In late 1987 Pantera brought about big changes with the dynamic of the group. The band introduced a new singer, nineteen-year-old Phil Anselmo. The band had begun a change from the familiar '80s glam rock, wear-as-much-spandex-as-you-could image into a very heavy metal (but undeniably Pantera) grungier style. My first introduction to Phil was at Joe's Garage: he walked over and grabbed me, dipping me down and kissing me. At the end of the night, he decided he was going to accompany me wherever I went. He rolled a joint and was passing it around the car, but I didn't take any. He said that if I didn't take a puff, he would make me pull the car over and fuck me. Um, I smoked some pot. We ended up at that chick's house, and when everyone started heading off to bed, Phil looked directly at me. "I am headed to bed if anyone would like to join me." I just smiled and said good night, not taking him up on the offer. I actually heard a rumor that the guys in Pantera had a bet going on how long it would take for all the local groupies to bed the new lead singer, and of course they had me in the running. And you know what the funny thing was? I wasn't the slut they thought I was. I had slept with hardly any of the people that they had thought I had. But even though it hurts a little bit, boys will be boys.

On another occasion, this chick I knew decided that we (that chick, Darrell, Phil, an Anthrax roadie's girlfriend, and I) were going to fly to Tulsa, Oklahoma, to party with Anthrax. Darrell had crafted these goggle-type sunglasses for us all to wear. He had cut up metallic stickers in lightning shapes and stuck them all over the lenses. I remember him saying that they would be the next big style. Darrell was so much fun to be around all the time, just a vibrant energy. He wore a baseball hat with the front flipped up, and he had written "just some dude" on it, and he wore it while he skateboarded through the airport. The flight was pretty sparse, peoplewise, but that didn't stop Darrell from engaging nearly every single person. If he was going to feel like a rock star, so would everyone else.

Linda, Rex Brown, & Darrell Abbott

Linda & Darrell Abbott

Phil Anselmo, Dime-Dime, & Darrell Abbott

Rex Brown, Vinnie Abbott, & Darrell Abbott

Rex Brown, Darrell Abbott, & Vinnie Abbott

There was an old man whom Darrell dubbed Popeye, and he actually did look a lot like him. But the most fun was a drunk dude, who fit right in with all the fun we were having. Darrell got everyone tossing a ball back and forth and also pouring beer out. Darrell, at the time, called himself Dime. This drunk made up a little ditty, saying, "Dime, Dime, I wish you were mine." It got so crazy during the flight that the pilot came out and, very cool-like, told us to settle down.

The Anthrax concert was incredible, and it was really cool to get to meet them all. Everyone stayed at the same hotel—in fact, we stayed in the same room. The whole weekend was unforgettable. Phil and I did try to start a relationship with each other, but it just wasn't in the cards. To be perfectly honest, I really wasn't completely comfortable with him. He always had a bit of an air about him, like he thought of himself as being better than or above everyone else.

By the time the '90s rolled around, the guys in Pantera were really making a name for themselves, touring all over the world. My husband and I ran into Darrell at a club in downtown Fort Worth, seeing Judas Priest. Vinnie was at home ill, so the whole time Darrell would hold up his cellphone so Vinnie could experience the concert as well. Through all the fame and fortune, the one thing that no one ever thought would happen did. Pantera broke up. Phil left the group. There were a lot of egos, and certain members of the band had started using heavy drugs. It just wasn't working anymore.

Everything sat dormant for quite some time until Vinnie and Darrell started another band called Damage Plan. They began building this band's success by going back to basics, playing the club circuit around the country.

I was in my mid- to late twenties and had begun to drift further away from everyone. I was working all the time and also taking classes at the local junior college. I just think at that point I was trying to start settling myself down, because inevitably I wanted to get married and have children. Vivian Campbell's lasting words to me rang through—that I was better than that life and should get away from it.

The last time I saw Darrell was at the Stormtroopers of Death (S.O.D.) concert. Debbie was dating the lead singer, Billy Milano, so my husband and I got to come to the show as VIP guests. While we were there, Darrell showed up. He looked so great and so very healthy! Darrell was so happy, and he even got up onstage with the band, having so much fun. No one could believe that we were getting to see Darrell with S.O.D. It was a memorable moment for everyone. I took my husband over to the bar so I could formally introduce him to Darrell. Doug, my husband, told me that Darrell ordered him a Black-Tooth Grin shot, held up the drink, and toasted, "You got the gold. You got the gold that everyone wanted, but you got her." Doug told Darrell, "Man, thanks, dude." At that very moment, I believe Doug might have understood why Darrell had always meant so much to me.

December 2004 was a school day, and I was up very early, getting lunches for the kids' school and trying to watch some of the early-morning news. It was at that moment I heard that Dimebag Darrell Abbott had been assassinated in Ohio during one of their shows. I stood there, tears filling my eyes, unable to move. It wasn't until I heard my husband's car pulling up in our driveway that I was able to move. I ran out the door and out to him, suddenly falling to my knees in a flood of tears. My husband wasn't supposed to be home yet, but he said when he saw it on the news at work all he could think about was getting home to me. He held me in his arms, comforting me, telling me how sorry he was over and over.

A part of my heart died the day Darrell was killed. I always thought that the day Randy Rhoads was killed in the plane crash was the day the music died, but it wasn't. December 8, 2004, was. This was something that I never would have imagined happening. Darrell was just the most wonderful, friendliest person. He was a legitimate rock star, but he didn't ever act like it. He always acted like a normal guy to everyone.

* * *

Darrell Lance Abbott
Born August 20, 1966
Died December 8, 2004

And believe it or not, just fourteen years later,
our Vinnie would die as well from cardiac arrest.
Vinnie Paul Abbott
Born March 11, 1964
Died June 22, 2018
RIP

Cut Too Short

Ozzy Osbourne & Randy Rhoads

While I had the opportunity to see in concert and meet Ozzy Osbourne as many as four times, all experiences unique in their own right, there will always only be one in particular that stands out above all others. It was Ozzy Osbourne and Motörhead. This was his first energy-charged tour with the infamous Randy Rhoads.

Going to concerts was somewhat tricky when we were younger—okay, underage. My parents were overprotective of me, but nothing in comparison with how protective Debbie's mom was with her. I even think she might have thought of me as a bad influence because Debbie was younger than I was. I believe we told her mom that we were going to the mall, where closing time was around 9:00 p.m., about the same time the concert would be over. We had my parents drop us off at the venue around 2:00 p.m., telling them that's when we would conduct our interviews with the bands.

Debbie and I had become very serious about printing a street magazine called *On the Road*, and Ozzy Osbourne was to be our big coming-out interview. CBS Records had been trying to contact Sharon Arden (Ozzy's manager and wife) all week long to clear our interview, but the day of the show arrived, and nothing was confirmed. Our fate was in our hands at this point, so we figured we would arrive early at the venue and cross our fingers.

Debbie & Linda on Ozzy Osbourne's tour bus

Randy Rhoads

When we got there, we were joined by the band's bus driver and Tommy Aldridge (Ozzy's drummer). They were both very friendly and quickly corralled us onto the tour bus, saying they were "protecting us" from Lemmy Kilmister of Motörhead. We were soon joined by Rudy Sarzo, who carried his bass guitar with him. He studiously plucked his bass while listening over his headphones. He noticed us staring intently and then offered his headphones so we could listen too. We were trying to contain our excitement, chatting like nervous Nellies because it was our first time to be on a tour bus with the band. We were soon joined by Randy Rhoads, whom Rudy described as "110 pounds when he's sopping wet." I just couldn't believe how friendly he was to us, considering he didn't even know us. He was just truly genuine. He was all smiles and full of a special kind of warmth. Everyone joked about Randy and his size, and he just smiled blushingly at their jokes—"He has to run around in the shower to get wet." He sat across from us and began discussing with enthusiasm *On the Road* and the dedication that it must take for us to try and do something like this. He was impressed, and his reassurance was what kept us going on. At some point he took my camera and snapped the infamous picture of Debbie and me sitting on the tour bus.

There was always plenty of activity going on backstage with the road crew continually working, but to even out all the work, there would be playtime too, especially when there were girls around to entertain. We watched a very large road-ie named Oz run head on into the front of the tour bus we were sitting in. The whole bus moved, and he continued until his head was busted open and bleeding. We also witnessed a truck and tour bus horn-blowing competition. I think our team won.

After the incredible show, they quickly made their way to the exit. A sweat-drenched and very tired Randy Rhoads paused, allowing us to take a quick picture. He made it a point to tell us that it was really nice to meet us. It is hard to put into words, and I don't imagine anyone will ever really know how much meeting Randy Rhoads meant to us. Meeting him would be a memory we would cherish for the rest of our lives. Randy Rhoads was killed in a plane crash on March 19, 1982. Truly, the day the music died for our generation.

* * *

RIP Randy Rhoads
Born December 6, 1956
Died March 19, 1982

Fangirl Moment

John Waite/Scandal
November 11, 1984, Dallas, Texas

I always had a huge crush on John Waite, even as far back as the Babys. Thanks to our promoter friend who set us up for complimentary tickets and backstage passes. He was actually setting us up to experience an amazing opportunity and made us believe that we *were* always in the right place at the right time. If you were lucky enough to be at the show, you would get the surprise of a lifetime. Eddie Van Halen would be joining both of the bands for impromptu jams. It's not every day that sort of thing happens. Eddie's new wife, Valerie Bertinelli, was best friends with Patty Smyth from Scandal.

During the show we began talking to a really adorable curly-haired guy who turned out to be Valerie's little brother, Patrick. I am not making this stuff up—it really happened like this for Debbie and me. Needless to say, after the concert we were invited back to the hotel for dinner and drinks with the entire Bertinelli family. Yep, good old mom and dad, brother Patrick, Valerie, and of course Eddie Van Halen. This was a pretty exciting invitation for a couple of silly girls, and it would be an invitation that we would not be turning down. We left the arena sadly without getting the opportunity to meet John Waite, but I have to admit I was sort of psyched to sit across the dinner table from Eddie and Valerie.

We arrived at the hotel and the desk clerk told us what floor the restaurant was on, so we proceeded over to the elevator. We stood there anxiously waiting for the elevator door to open, and then…it opened. Oh my God…there he was… John Waite. If my eyes had not been attached to my head they would have rolled out onto the floor. My mouth was agape. My heart was pounding. One million clever words were rushing through my mind, but by God nothing would come out except one guttural grunt. Debbie watched the train wreck unfold without even a nudge to bring me back from my stupor. John was so gracious, and he smiled *so sexily* at me. Then he tilted his head over so sweetly and said, "Excuse me, darling," then slipped by us out into the night. Debbie pulled me onto the elevator laughing at me: "Oh boy, you looked like a dumbass!" I couldn't believe it, the moment I dreamed about over and over as a young girl. It was a damn silly moment, but it defined my life for a few years after that. I never again had another fangirl moment about anyone.

The Most Romantic Moment of My Life

Dio
November 14, 1984 & November 17, 1985

How could you love someone with so much of your entire being and have to realize that they wouldn't ever know? I am about to tell you one of my most important stories that so deeply impacted my life. So, while you are reading about all of the adventure, danger, crazy antics, discovery and hilarious moments don't forget that someone's heart ended up never to be fulfilled.

Of course the story starts out with three groupies scamming to meet and hang out with the heavy metal legend Dio and his band. The three groupies are Linda, Debbie and Lenise. Who else would I be writing about? We knew the band was in Dallas for a show on November 14th, so on a hunch that they might be in town early, we headed to search the area to try and find out where they might be staying. We had learned that you could usually drive and with careful investigation figure out where the band was staying. Well, we saw unnatural disturbances such as trucks and tour buses in the area around The Greenleaf Hotel, right off of I-30. We figured this was as good a place as any to start our search so we entered the hotel and went directly to the hotel bar. The hotel bar and the waitresses who work there are the perfect persons to speak to if you want to know what is going on in or around the area. We ordered drinks and began getting in close with the waitress, finally feeling comfortable enough we just asked her if the band had been to the bar yet. "Yes, they have but decided to go out to eat." We smiled so mischievously as she continued to explain. "They went to…I think Radcliffes' Restaurant." We thanked her, left her a hefty tip and left searching for the restaurant. Radcliffes' is a five star restaurant in Dallas Texas, and we panicked about not being able to even afford a drink there, but we took our chances. By this time, we had pretty much learned that being three hot women dressed to the nine, could pretty much get what we wanted with a little flirting. Luckily things came to us reasonably easy. We told the host that we were friends with the band who was eating there and asked to be seated near their table because we were friends and wanted to surprise them and of course the host made it happen for us. We were sitting in perfect view of the band. We wanted to seem legit, so we ordered a salad and a couple of drinks. Okay, maybe more than a couple of drinks. For some reason, out of the fucking blue, I decided to take a drag off of Lenise's cigarette. Why? Because I didn't smoke. Now as many of you already know, if you have never smoked a cigarette before the effects are often not very good. Well that was an understatement for me. I think I turned five shades of purple and the room began spinning around. Oh shit! This sucks! And wouldn't you know, it was at this point in time we sent a bottle of Dom Perignon over to their table. When the champagne arrived, they all turned around finally noticing us sitting there waving seductively at them. I don't know if I looked seductive, because I still felt rather purple. The waiter came to our table "Ladies, the Gentlemen at that table would like for you to come and join them." We smiled, accepting the invitation and proceeded to move over to the table. The greeting was so sweet. They shuffled around and made room for us to sit at the table with them. It didn't take long to figure out that these guys were really very nice, not your typical rock stars. It was a really nice change, but it sort of left us to experience an environment that we hadn't yet experienced. I was feeling worse for wear and decided to excuse myself to the restroom, and as I approached the restroom I was greeted by Vivian Campbell. He was probably the most attractive man I had ever laid eyes on, and my heart began to pound. He gently took my hands and asked, "Are you alright?" Irish accent! Irish accent! Oh my God, I was doomed! I explained to him that I wasn't feeling quite well. He caressed my hands and said, "Don't worry darling, I will look out after you tonight." He let go of my hands and let me go on to the restroom, where I proceeded to HURL every single thing I had put into my stomach from that entire day. Geez, I sort of felt a bit better. Still drunk, but better. I went back to the table and he had my chair moved beside him and he had gotten me a cup of coffee. I had never drank coffee before, but at that moment it was wonderful and actually just what I needed. Suddenly I was being questioned by Ronnie Jame Dio from the far end of the table. "How old are you?" He didn't ask anyone else that, only me. I glanced at Vivian sensing there might have been some sort of issue in the past, but I proceeded to answer politely, "I am twenty one." There was a slight giggling and mumbling around the table, and Ronnie smiled again. "Can I see your Identification or Driver's License?" I nodded and watched as it passed through everyone at the table, checking to make sure. No one believed me, but I did have proof. Finally Vivian leaned over. "I'm twenty one also." I was totally enamored by him. I couldn't stop looking at him. He was so precious. Everyone continued to converse, until finally decided it was time to return back to the Hotel. Vivian took my hand and asked for me to join him there. Like DUH! I wasn't going to let him get away from me that easily. I politely nodded, yes.

It had begun to storm outside. The band left in their limousine, and we piled into Lenise's little car. At this point it started to rain a torrential downpour, and we became scared as Lenise tried navigating the streets. You could barely see 3 feet ahead of you, when all of a sudden Lenise hit something. We screamed bloody murder! We didn't know what she hit. "Should we stop?" We screamed NO! We convinced ourselves it was some sort of sawhorse barricade in the middle of the road and when she hit it, it went up and over the car. Yeah, that was it. We were silent the whole drive back to the Hotel, and by the time we made it into the Hotel we were also soaked to the bone. We looked like drowned rats. Embarrassed, we made our way up to the Hotel bar. Vivian turned and immediately said, "Awe, you're soaked." He took my hands and led me out of the bar to the elevator. "We've got to get you out of those wet clothes." I didn't have anything with me to change into so I figured this was when he turned into that rock star type and put the move on me. He didn't. He took a pair of blue jeans and a pink sweatshirt out of his suitcase and lay them on the bed. "We look about the same size, maybe they'll fit you." I picked up the clothes and turned to go to the restroom. "Wait!" He said. "Change here." Oh God! My heart was pounding so fast, as I slowly undressed in front of him. He sat on the bed, and as I stood naked in front of him he uttered. "Absolutely beautiful." I slowly exhaled the breath that I had been holding in and quickly put on the clothes. They fit me! I don't mean, sort of fit me. They fit me exactly! We were the exact same size. We were both shocked, grabbed each other's hand and left back to the bar. Everyone was talking and having a great time. The waitress walked over to me and said, "I see you found them." I grinned and nodded my head. Vivian grinned as well, realizing that we had planned out the whole evening to work in our favor. I think he was pretty happy we had. Eventually the party moved to Ronnie James Dio's room, where everyone began smoking marijuana and drinking. Vivian and I arrived at the room, opened the door and a large billowing cloud of smoke engulfed us. We walked in and mingled about. Debbie and Ronnie were having what seemed to be a smoke off. Lenise was talking to this really good looking man dressed in a three piece suit. Everyone seemed to be really happy. Vivian took my hand and led me over the sliding door that led out to the balcony. We walked outside and he pulled the door shut, then turned to me. He took me into his arms and we began to kiss. I had never been kissed with so much feeling and passion.

I felt as if I was floating. A photographer had started snapping pictures of us. Vivian and I turned to him, giving him the look of not wanting to be disturbed. The photographer laughed, "Alright. Alright." He pulled the curtain closed and Vivian and I began kissing again. I feel like it doesn't matter how hard I try to explain how I was feeling, you wouldn't understand. It was the single most romantic moment of my entire life. It was cool outside from the rain, but I felt so warm. The Dallas City skyline was barely visible due to the misting rain. It was a Harlequin Moment. I didn't want it to end, but the breeze outside shifted and the mist began to hit us. He took my hand and we left for his room. I was certain that we would end up making love all night long, but once we got to his room he asked if I wanted to sleep in the other bed or with him. I was confused. "You." I uttered. He stripped down, crawled into bed. I did the same and as I moved towards him, he shoved a King sized pillow down in between us. "Don't be a bed hog now." He said, making sure I understood that his side was his, and mine was mine. It was the first time that anyone had ever done something like this with me. I didn't know what to do, except just go to sleep and I did.

The next morning I woke up before him. I didn't want to wake him, so I got up and left. Lenise had left sometime the night before, leaving Debbie and I behind with the band. I called her from the pay phone to come and pick us up, then I located Debbie. We waited downstairs for Lenise to arrive, then we went home. I didn't really want to talk to Debbie about it, because originally the plan was for Debbie to meet

and hook up with Vivian but because the plan changed I figured she was a little pissed at me. In fact, I don't think we
talked about it for many many years after that. I just figured it
was best that way. There wasn't any type of agreement like guys
have such as bros before hoes. I don't know what they would
call it if there was.

I washed Vivian's clothes and folded them neatly. In the afternoon, I called the Hotel and asked for Vivian's room. Once
connected, Vivian said "You left…" I told him I had some
things I needed to do and we were planning to come to the
show tonight. He sat us up with Complimentary tickets and
backstage passes. We agreed to see each other later that night
then let each other go.

We thought it was really odd that Lenise had chosen not
to go to the show, so I drove. Debbie said she had spent the
evening conversing with Claude, where nothing happened.
I nodded saying how I spent the evening with Vivian, and how
romantic he was. Once we arrived at the arena, we found our
seats next to all of the executives and record personnel. Excitement was in the air. Dokken was the opening act, and they
were quite good. I could hardly contain my excitement to see
Vivian, and it wasn't long before the lights dimmed and there
he was looking like some sort of GOD on that stage. I was
getting so insanely aroused, and could barely wait to see him
backstage and as soon as the show was over I couldn't get back
there quick enough. I was dressed in a dress and heels tonight.
I wanted to impress him and let him know I didn't look like
a drowned rat all of the time. We were standing backstage,

and he walked in. He walked past all the fans and straight to me, taking my hand and leading me to a table. We sat down. "I'm so embarrassed I tripped on stage." He said, half blushing. My eyes widened. "Are you kidding me? You were absolutely amazing!" The fans started clambering around him and I. He apologized. I smiled at him. "They are your fans, it's really alright." He began signing autographs, taking pictures and in between he would lean in giving me kisses. I felt like a Queen at that very moment, and he was my King. I never wanted this moment to end. After the fans began to trickle down, Vivian looked over to me. "Did your friend come to the show tonight?" I shook my head no. "Did she tell you what she did last night?" I was curious, shaking my head no. Vivian went on to explain in between the laughter that Lenise and one of the management team were getting along really well, so they went out to the bus. At that time the dude went over to a cabinet and took out sexual Sadomasochism instrumentation laying it all out on the table. My eyes are widening, knowing now why she hadn't said anything to us about what all had happened the night before. Vivian continued telling me. Lenise (obviously panicking in her mind) supposedly looked down at the stuff and quickly turned it around on the dude. "Yea, I like that shit but I like to go first." Needless to say he was down to whatever she wanted to do, so Lenise tied this man up to the unremovable table and benches on the bus and proceeded to leave. Vivian was laughing so hard, as I began to laugh as well. Vivian said that even Ronnie James Dio agreed that this was the greatest and funniest tour story that had ever happened and it would go down in the annals of Rock and Roll history. Lenise was obviously one cool cucumber, and she had outdid herself on this one. What a classic story!

We waited a bit longer and decided it was time to leave, agreeing to meet each other over at the Hotel. Debbie didn't really want to, but I wasn't going to walk away from Vivian yet. I knew that moment was coming, but I wanted our time to last as long as it could.

Once we got back to his room we talked for a bit. He talked about the tour ending and making a trip to Ireland for the holidays, and he skirted around the possibility of me being with him. I wanted to be with, forever. I never wanted to leave his side. It was time to make the biggest decision of my life. I sighed and said no. I explained that my family would be disappointed in me if I up and left and not attended our family festivities. My heart was breaking. I knew inside what the real reason was, why I couldn't leave with him. I wanted more for my life. I wanted a husband I could count on with faithfulness. I wanted a home with children. Could I ever really have something like this with a man like Vivian? I didn't think so, at the time. We hugged each other and began to get undressed, and crawled into the bed. He smiled, waving his finger at me. "Don't be a bed hog." He lifted the King pillow in between us once more. We lay there talking until a knock came on the door. It was Debbie. She was demanding that we leave. I didn't want to leave him, but he urged me to go ahead and go. So I did. I couldn't believe I walked away from him. I didn't know if I would ever see him again.

Remembrances of my deep, whole hearted love for Vivian raced through my mind every single day. It seemed that every time I thought about him, the Kenny Loggins song, "Forever" would come on the radio. I decided this was my song, the one song which related to this special and painful moment in my life. "Forever" so humanly down to earth, so eloquently unfolding my desires, describing my dream that became a reality. My reality that literally slipped through my fingers to become only a dream once again.

There wasn't one day that I didn't think of him. I wondered if I would ever see him again. He was a full fledged rock star now, photographs in all the magazines. I wondered if he would even remember me. One day I picked up the newspaper and noticed that Dio would be coming back to town November 17th, almost one year to the day. I would finally get to see him again. I also noticed that Vivian would be doing an autograph signing party at a Dallas record store. This was my perfect opportunity. I was nervous, but I had to do it. This friend of mine went with me to the autograph signing, and we stood for hours waiting in line with the fans. Finally it was my turn and I stepped up. Vivian looked up directly at me and a huge smile came across his face and he blurted out. "LINDA!" A huge smile came across my face and I hurried over, and we moved into each other's arms. We chatted for a second then he told me his hotel and room number, asking me to call him. It was as simple as that, but I couldn't help but feel nervous like something was up. Later that day I nervously placed the phone call. It rang once, twice then three times when finally a woman answered the phone. "May I speak to Vivian?" "No, you may not. He said to tell you that he has put you on the list." My heart sank. What was happening? I don't understand. Once I was alone, I cried.

A friend of mine accompanied me to the show, and afterwards we went backstage. Vivian came into the room, but avoided me for the longest time. I had enough and I decided to leave, but he quickly came over taking my arm. "Don't leave yet." "Why?" He explained that he had to give the fans ample amount of attention and urged me to wait so I waited. He finally came over, took my hand leading me to a table where we sat down. He looked into my eyes. "I got married." My heart sank. "Why didn't you just tell me?" "I didn't want to hurt you." "Too late." A moment of silence filled the large room. He took my hands. "I could never forget my bed hog." I looked into his eyes as mine filled with tears. He suddenly looked at me very seriously. "Linda, you are so very sweet. This life is just not for you. You are better than this. There is more for you, better things for you. Do you understand?" I looked into his eyes and nodded. "Yes." He took my hand and we walked out into the hallway where several people snapped pictures, then he turned to me. "I have to go now." I looked into his eyes, then he suddenly pulled me over to an empty room. He pushed me against the wall and began to kiss me passionately, then he quickly turned and left walking out of my life forever. I couldn't help but cry. At that very moment I honestly didn't think I could ever love someone like I felt love for him.

Vivian Campbell & Linda
Photo Credit: Michael Insuante

Vivian Campbell, Linda, & Michael Insuante
Photo Credit: Michael Insuante

Linda, Vivian Campbell, & The Monk
Photo Credit: The Monk

Ronnie James Dio & Linda

We are both now 60 years old, and we have both lived a lifetime. He went on to have complete fame and fortune, taking his career into the Stratosphere. He had two children with his wife and they were married for at least 30 years. He divorced and is now married to another woman. What about me, you ask? I met a wonderful man, the actual man of my dreams. We have been happily married for 30 plus years. We had two perfect children. I had all my dreams come true with my husband.

Do I ever think about Vivian? Of course I do. I'm only human. I guess some part of me will always love him, but definitely not like I love my husband. To be honest, Vivian changed my life. He was the one person that saw who I really was, what was really right for me. If he hadn't pushed me to get away from that life, I don't know if I ever would have. If I hadn't I wouldn't have met my wonderful husband. So in a way, I guess you could say I owe him. I put Vivian on my bucket list, simply because I want to have that moment to tell him 'thank you.' Thank you for telling me that life wasn't for me. Thank you for knowing who I really was inside, when I don't think I even knew.

Maybe someday…I will get that chance and maybe when he sees me he just might remember.

Addition to the story…I took my husband to the Dio concert in 2002-2003 and we were able to get backstage to see everyone. The moment that Ronnie James Dio saw me, his eyes lit up and he belted out "LINDA!!!" He remembered me. I introduced him to my husband whom he fell in love with.

Ronnie James Dio was the most wonderful and nicest man that I ever met, being a legendary Rock Star and all. He was so kind and so sweet. I feel lucky to have had the opportunity to have been a little piece of his life.

Ronnie James Dio passed away May 16, 2010 from cancer. I will never forget you.

Deep Purple/Giuffria

January 25, 1985
Reunion Arena

W hat better way to get over my broken heart than to quickly jump right back onto the rock star? Oh shit, I mean bicycle. Haha! We decided to go to the Deep Purple concert. I think the actual objective was supposed to be Giuffria, because Greg Giuffria used to be in a group called Angel, and they were all pretty hot. We knew the promoter for the show, and he gladly set us up with complimentary tickets and backstage passes.

I guess we really didn't know what we were getting ourselves into as we walked through the audience because the crowd looked to be a bit of an older generation. I guess that makes sense, since Deep Purple was formed in 1968, so they were on the tail end of the hippie period in time. To be honest, I really didn't know that much at all about Deep Purple. They had a lot of hit songs, but they just didn't play them on the radio much. My brothers were into them, and I think that is how I even knew who they were.

We were walking around when a gentleman with a laminated pass approached us. "Excuse me," he said. He was one of the crew members from Deep Purple, and he told us we would be welcome to come and stand up on the monitor-and-lighting platform, which sat out on the floor in the middle of the audience, almost directly in front of the stage. Okay, this was different. Usually no one, especially groupies, was allowed on this. It was pretty much reserved for very important persons, so I guess for some reason we had become very important persons. Go figure. Let me start off by saying that the show was absolutely phenomenal! They were really good! They were very talented! They were *men*! They weren't young rock star boys but men. Super sexy! I admit that I was definitely turned on. They had two songs ("Perfect Strangers" and "Knocking at Your Back Door"), and they were packed with a lot of sexual energy. I really was interested in what I was seeing.

We thought we would just be heading home after the show because it didn't seem like anything was going to happen with Giuffria. The guy who had let us stand up on the platform escorted us to a large backstage room. "Make yourselves comfortable." We sort of stood there and glanced around at one another, feeling a bit confused. What are we supposed to do? The room was decked out to the hilt, classy, much like a rich person's living area. It had comfy couches. The tables were covered with tablecloths. There was good food, like healthy food, on the tables. This wasn't a normal backstage area, or none like we had ever experienced. There was wine, along with champagne. What the hell was going on? This must be another strange backstage event like the Van Halen Mexican party. To say that we felt a little bit out of place was an understatement, but we could pull it off, or at least I hoped that we could. Suddenly the door opened, and the members of Deep Purple slowly came into the room. They were dressed in plush purple robes and slippers. I don't know about Lenise and Debbie, but I felt almost dumbfounded. Other people came into the room with them, people in nice dresses and suits and a few like us, normals. They began to mingle among the crowd, talking about business, their estates in London, the latest cars and music. I was standing alone at first until maestro Jon Lord walked over and ran his fingers through his hair. "I must have myself a haircut. I don't want to be mistaken for those Iron Maiden boys." I grinned. Then I sat down on a couch by myself as I sipped a glass of champagne. I was quite nervous until all of a sudden Ian Gillan, the lead singer of Deep Purple, sat down beside me—then I panicked. I smiled sweetly at him, and he told me I looked absolutely lovely, laying his hand gently on my knee. I thanked him, and his hand stayed on my knee while people would come and chat with him. I didn't know what to think or what to do except to sit there and be polite. He leaned over to me and whispered, "I must go dress now. We are preparing to go to the hotel." He paused a minute, gazing deep into my eyes. "I do hope you plan on meeting us there, yes?" I nodded yes and watched as he left the room. I met back up with Lenise and Debbie and found out they were being romanced as well by other members, and they were in unison that we indeed would be going to the hotel. Why on earth would we turn something like this down? No way!

Lenise, Debbie, and I just thought we had seen it all until we made our way over to the hotel. First off, this wasn't just any hotel. This hotel was completely made of marble. I don't remember the name of it, but I think it's called the Renaissance

Hotel now. It had a private lounge where refined men could sit sipping brandy, smoke fat stogies, and play intelligent games like chess. What an experience! I nervously sat next to Debbie, and we observed everyone in the room. Oh my God! It was Ritchie Blackmore! He was sitting right by us, and I could feel his legendary vibes. "I gotta go pee," I whispered to Debbie. I stood up and was starting to walk past Ian Gillan, who was playing chess with another gentleman, when he reached over, taking my arm and gently pulling me down to him. "Do you give good back rubs?" he whispered into my ear. I'll swear chills passed all over me. I almost blurted out, "Oh yeah, I give great back rubs!" Thank God I didn't and had more couth to simply say, "Yes, I believe so."

He told me that as soon as I returned from the restroom, we would leave for his bedroom. He held my arm around his as we left for his room, and I gotta tell you, I was really liking being treated like this. Once we arrived in his room, he went directly to the room phone and ordered Dom Pérignon champagne and pâté; then he stripped down naked right in front of me. I would say that he was probably in his early forties, and he didn't look bad at all, let me tell you. My heart sank when he turned to me. "Come along now, take off your clothes as well."

My eyes widened, and I swallowed hard. "Uh, no."

He explained how he was a full nudist and said he understood if I was a bit shy but that he would get me naked. He went to his suitcase and took out a fishnet-type tank shirt and tossed it over to me, explaining this would make the transition easier for me. Who was he kidding? No it wouldn't! But he was very insistent, so I stripped down to my panties and the fishnet shirt. The room service arrived, and Ian answered the door completely naked as the tray was rolled into the room; then he tipped the waiter as he left. We sat on the balcony, sipping champagne and eating pâté, talking for a bit. The pâté sucked ass, but I wasn't going to complain. He was romantic, looping our arms together as we sipped the champagne, and I giggled. He stood and led me back into the room, turning and lifting the net shirt over my head, throwing it to the ground. He stepped back a bit, and his eyes widened. "My God, sweetheart, you absolutely have the most beautiful breasts." I could have fainted. From that point on, the fact that Ian Gillan had said I had the "most beautiful breasts" would be my new claim to fame.

We lay back on the bed and began to kiss until we were interrupted by a rapid knock on the door. He stood and answered the door, and it was Debbie. She seemed a bit in a panic. She explained that Ian Paice was freaking her out and she wanted to leave. Ian took her hand and led her into the room, and needless to say we weren't alone anymore, but it didn't really make a difference. Debbie and I had been in situations like this before, and it really didn't bother us. We were all kissing when yet another rapping (more like banging) came at the door, and at the same time the phone rang. Ian quickly instructed us to be quiet as he opened the door and answered the phone, saying hello to *his wife*!!! Debbie and I quickly looked at each other. "OH SHIT!" We quickly put on our clothing and ran to Lenise at the door, quickly leaving while Ian was on the phone with his wife.

Lenise was pissed at us. We were supposed to meet at one point and leave for Austin, Texas, around 8:00 a.m. to go to the KISS concert. It was 4:00 a.m. already. I thought, Hell! Let's just go now! We did, driving all the way to Austin and getting a little motel once we arrived to sleep it off.

We rushed out of the grandiose Wyndham Hotel after an incredible evening of partying "grown-up style" with the legendary Deep Purple, hitting the road to Austin, Texas. Um, yeah, that's another story for another chapter.

The Shoes Didn't Fit

KISS
January 26, 1985

After arriving in Austin, Texas, we checked ourselves into a small little motel reasonably close to the arena and crashed out for some much needed rest. At 8:00 p.m. we arrived at the arena for a much-anticipated KISS concert. We were dressed to the hilt with every intention that we would get seen, except for one thing. I had forgotten my high-heeled shoes for my outfit, so it was either wear my tenny shoes or borrow a pair of shoes from Lenise or Debbie. The problem with that was that I wore only a size six, and they both wore size nine. I decided to be a trouper and make it work, stuffing the toes of the shoes with Kleenex and wearing the larger size.

We were under the impression that our backstage passes and tickets would be waiting for us at will call, but it was a major letdown realizing our connection didn't pull through. So there we were, in a different town, knowing no one, and with an insufficient amount of money. Lenise had money, so she blew Debbie and me off and bought herself a ticket and went inside to enjoy the show. Debbie and I didn't have enough money to get ourselves tickets, so we were left to deal with the whole situation on our own, and we had no idea what to do. For a while we dealt with the unwanted advances and bargaining from countless roadies to no avail. We were feeling pretty hopeless and felt that it just couldn't get any worse. Yes. Yes, it could. It started to rain, which contributed to making us look like two drowned rats. We were huddled together when suddenly we noticed a stretch limousine slowly driving our way. My first thought was "No way." Did I mention how things like this tended to happen to Debbie and me? The limousine pulled to a complete stop very close to us. The darkened backseat window slowly rolled down, and a hand extended outward, with a finger beckoning us to come there. We grasped our hands together and walked over. The driver stepped out and opened the door and motioned for us to get in. We leaned down to finally get a view of just who was in that limousine, and in that very instant it became clear. It was Gene Simmons, the bass guitarist—"the Demon"—of KISS. I was very excited, but Debbie completely slipped into a manic fit, repeating over and over, "Oh my God!" Gene Simmons graciously invited us to join him, so we sat on each side. Debbie ran her hands reverently over his body as if he were a deity that had stepped down from Olympus just to be in our presence. Debbie kept repeating over and over, "Oh my God!"

Gene looked over to me and asked, "Is she going to be all right?"

I smiled and said, "Yes," completely understanding where Debbie was coming from at that moment. In a sense she was looking at her god (her god of thunder) face to face. As a young girl, Debbie had had her bedroom walls and ceiling plastered with enormous superposters, going to sleep every single night gazing at him and having him engulf her dreams. This was her moment, and I was going to make sure that neither I nor even Gene Simmons was going to take this moment away from her.

Needless to say, Gene made sure that we were treated like the groupie queens we were, slapping VIP backstage passes on us and making sure we were set up where we could see the whole show. It was a fantastic show! I couldn't help but reflect on the previous KISS concerts we had attended, and if you had asked me then if I thought we would ever get to meet and hang out with the band…You know what? I would have told you yes. We always got what we wanted.

We finally met up with Lenise backstage, because of course we got her a backstage pass too. Outside the arena, we began talking with some young Hispanic males, absolutely adorable and very sure of themselves. They kept telling us they were members of the Hispanic pop group Menudo. We received directions from KISS to meet them at the hotel, and Debbie nervously left upstairs for her big "date" with Gene Simmons. Lenise and I weren't quite ready to call it a night, so we went to grab a drink or two at the hotel bar. We were already half lit from the drinks we had at the concert, but that didn't stop us from loading up on more booze. The more booze we drank, the funnier our conversations became. We began talking about pussy queefs. Why? I don't know why. We began making the sounds of pussy queefs at our small table, actually beginning to make a scene. We suddenly looked up to see Bruce Kulick, who was the current guitarist for KISS. Poor Bruce. He had no idea what he had walked into. He was exceptionally friendly and polite, and it wasn't until years later that I actually felt embarrassed by our behavior. I wondered (but doubted) whether his intention was to try and get laid, but I can tell you we were too blitzed for something like that to happen. We said our goodbyes, and Lenise and I went back to our motel. We both crashed face first on our beds but were jolted back up by a banging on the door. "What the hell?" we thought. Okay, you could say that our little adventure had already been strange enough, but you would be wrong. Lenise opened the door to see those young Hispanic boys (supposedly from Menudo) standing there with grins from ear to ear. Had they been following us the entire night??? Whatever they thought was going to happen wasn't. Lenise let out a loud, hysterical laugh and then slammed the door in their faces.

The next day we left before checkout and headed to pick Debbie up from the hotel where she had spent the night with Gene Simmons. We didn't want to laugh, but we couldn't help it when we saw her straggling down the sidewalk. We ribbed her all the way home. The moment we got back to our apartment in Arlington, Texas, Debbie rushed upstairs to call her mother. "I fucked Gene Simmons!" she exclaimed. I am not exactly sure how her mom responded, but she was one cool lady. I am sure she responded with something like "That's nice. I hope you made him wear a condom."

So one of the advantages of seeing and meeting KISS in Austin, Texas, was that we had the upper hand over all the groupies in Dallas, Texas. We were already set up with VIP backstage passes, along with complimentary tickets. In Austin, I had taken a liking to Paul Stanley's guitar technician. They called him Romeo, and for good reason. He was very handsome and very nice. From the moment we met in Austin, Texas, Romeo and I had a very close connection, and we would spend every moment possible with each other while he was in town. Every time KISS came to town, I would automatically be set up. It was nice. It made up for a lot of fun things happening. One time when KISS came through, we were invited to have dinner at the arena before the show. It was so funny. Gene Simmons (being the ultimate showman) was sitting across from us at the table, and while chewing, he would stick his tongue out, showing us all the food. We would all giggle and squeal, which I am sure was the reaction he was hoping for. One of the other advantages to knowing the "right" persons was that we would always be escorted out to the front row before the show would start, usually directly in front of Gene Simmons. So during the show tons of confetti would be blown out of a loud-sounding cannon, raining down on everyone and everywhere. A roadie would usually be the one to use a lawn blower to blow all the confetti off the stage, but to our surprise this particular time it would be Gene Simmons. He walked onto the stage and, while looking directly at us with a mischievous demon smirk, flicked the lawn blower on and blew all the confetti out onto us. Debbie and I spent hours cleaning confetti out of every orifice of our bodies, even our ears.

It was really fun having this type of connection with the band. I saw and met KISS nine times from 1977 to 1988, and that span of eleven years was completely packed with wonderful memories.

Gene Simmons

Eric Carr

"You're Wrecked!"

Lemmy Kilmister

Let's face it—this book would be nothing without a chapter for Lemmy Kilmister. However, I sat for days trying to figure out how to write down all my adventures and how I felt about him. It definitely wasn't the easiest thing to put into words. Truth is, for years I wasn't entirely sure how I felt about Lemmy. He was sort of mysterious and kind of scary. I was afraid to let my guard down with him. It took some time for me to discover that I really loved him. Lemmy was a unique character, one of a kind, and a very, very sweet individual. He was my friend.

The first time I ever found out who Lemmy was was in 1981, when Motörhead opened up for Ozzy Osbourne. Rudy Sarzo and Tommy Aldridge had pretty much painted Lemmy as a monster or something, quickly herding us onto their tour bus to "protect" us from him, they said. So we absolutely had no interaction with him or anyone from Motörhead, for that matter, but I did make it out front during the show and managed to get some very good photographs. Motörhead's style of music was insane, and I had never heard music played that loud or that fast before. At this period of time, Debbie's and my musical taste was pretty innocent, and we had not yet been introduced to many different styles, but that time would come.

Motörhead's music had definitely planted a seed in our mind, and we wanted more of that sound, so on November 28, 1984, we decided to go see Mercyful Fate, Motörhead, and Exciter at the Bronco Bowl. We had no idea what we were getting ourselves into, going to this concert. The bands were not glammed up and were also very down to earth, which was very different from what we were used to. Glam bands used more hair spray than Debbie or I could use in an entire year.

It wasn't unusual that we arrived at the arena early. We had discovered in past situations that it was a good way to get ahead of all the other groupies, as well as possibly get the chance to run into one of the band members. We were quickly approached by Mercyful Fate's manager, and he asked us if we had the resources to take Mercyful Fate to their autograph-signing party in Arlington, Texas. What? Are you kidding me? YES! Lenise quickly jumped and accepted King Diamond riding with her, and if you knew her, you would understand how appropriate that was. Debbie and I had Kim Ruzz and the manager in our car. On the way there, Lenise was pulled over by the police for speeding. King Diamond was in full black-and-white makeup, dressed in black, with a black cape and a huge silver upside-down cross hanging around his neck, so you can imagine the officer's face when he leaned down and saw him in Lenise's passenger seat. Needless to say, he let them go when he found out the details. We arrived at the record store Pipe Dreams for the autograph-signing party, and in front of all of our friends, King Diamond and Kim Ruzz stepped out of our cars. Amazing moment. While the autograph party was going on, I assisted the manager in getting an express letter sent, which I believe contained immigration papers.

Later that night, at the arena, we proceeded backstage and entered into a room full of wild and rough-looking musicians wandering around with Jack Daniels bottles in hand. Almost immediately we were confronted by the guitarist Phil Campbell and the "infamous" Lemmy Kilmister, and they quickly directed all their attention to us, keeping us in stitches the entire time. Lemmy kept doing impressions and worked very hard on getting us drunk. Lemmy and Phil wanted to go to this club called the Ritz, so we offered to take them in my car. On the way there, Lemmy kept making me drink what he called "Lemmy juice," which I think was a mixture of orange juice, vodka, and some other unknown ingredient. I was extremely nervous because I was driving every one of our friends' heavy metal heroes, and I was definitely on the way to being very drunk. I felt the weight of the world on my shoulders as my car slammed into a huge pothole, and it seemed as if my car lifted and gracefully floated through the air, then comfortably landed in the correct lane, directly on track. I glanced at Debbie, and she knew exactly what I was thinking: "OH SHIT!!!!" I actually had the feeling of standing right next to pyrotechnics going off and feeling that sheet of sweat pour over you. I was so relieved to finally make it to the Ritz. I had time to get sobered up before I had to drive them to their hotel. Everyone knew who they were, and we all were escorted in for free. The whole night we danced while Lemmy and Phil played pool.

At the end of the night, we ended up in Lemmy's hotel room, listening to the Everly Brothers, and I passed out. Debbie had gone with Phil to his room, and when I woke up, I was alone with Lemmy in his room. I won't lie and say I wasn't scared to death. This was the man that Rudy Sarzo and Tommy Aldridge thought they had to protect me from. It didn't take me long to learn that Lemmy was a decent man, and he didn't try anything with me. Instead we sat there and read books together until the wee hours of the morning. Then I left. I returned the next day to pick up Debbie. We sat in Phil's room laughing and talking for a bit until we went next door to say goodbye to Lemmy. The next night Debbie went back to party with Phil one more time, but this time she took Motörhead's biggest fans, Casey and Harden from Rigor Mortis. I didn't go the second night. Debbie said Lemmy was at the bar but seemed real "doomed up," finally getting up to go to his room, saying he was "feeling his age."

I sat at the apartment, feeling regret that I didn't go and spend another night with him, and I really don't know why I didn't go.

We would see Motörhead again on October 25, 1986, when they would be headlining their own tour with the opening acts Wendy O. Williams and Cro-Mags. All the guys remembered us immediately, and it was so much fun hanging around with them again. Lemmy seemed so happy to see me, showering me with gifts. He gave me a pin, a T-shirt, a rare album, a laminated pass, and a newspaper with an article on Motörhead in it. Debbie and I accompanied Lemmy on the tour bus back to the Doubletree Inn for him to pick something up. I had already been drinking quite a bit, and I barfed at the hotel. I was so embarrassed, and I kept apologizing. He smiled, hugging me, then signed an autograph to me saying, "You're not drunk! You're wrecked!" I still have it to this day. We went back to the arena and Lemmy told me that during the shows he wanted me to be standing on the stage to the side. He showed me the area, then gave me a sweet hug and went backstage to get ready for the show. Debbie and I turned to see Wendy O. Williams standing there glaring at me. She was so absolutely frightening I'll swear my asshole clinched. She walked closer and growled at me, "You're not his type, little girl." I shrugged and was interrupted by Lemmy, who stuck his head out of his dressing room. "Leave her alone, Wendy!" I was very thankful he had the intuition to check on me. From that point on I just kept my distance from Wendy. That night, Lemmy dedicated "Steal your Face" to Debbie and me onstage. They had to leave that night, so we didn't get to spend any quality one-on-one time together.

I didn't see Motörhead again until August 13, 2003. I hadn't seen Lemmy in approximately eighteen years. I had gotten married. I had children. It literally seemed as if I had lived a lifetime since the last time I had seen Lemmy. How would Lemmy possibly remember me? I thought that about Ronnie James Dio, but it happened to be at this show in particular he immediately remembered me, grinning like a Cheshire cat.

My husband and I had tickets, but I didn't have any backstage passes. I told my husband there was a very good chance

I could get us backstage passes if we drove over a bit early, and I just might see someone I knew. Once we got to the arena, I told my husband I needed to go alone for a chance of getting the passes, and he agreed. I trotted through the gate undetected and began to walk around, hoping to find someone I might know. I started around a corner and ran smack dab into Lemmy. His eyes widened. "Linda?"

I shook my head with a grin. "Lemmy," I said, throwing my arms around him, hugging him tightly. "How could you possibly remember me after all these years?"

He reached over, tapping my nose. "Linda, I will never forget you." I believed him. Lemmy never lied, always saying exactly what he meant.

"Love you, Lemmy," I said to him, looking deep into his eyes. He set us up with tickets and backstage passes without even questioning me. The show was absolutely incredible. During the Iron Maiden show, we went backstage, and as we were entering through the gate, I saw Lemmy as he was leaving. He looked directly at me and held his hand up, waving goodbye to me. I tried to hurry through the gate, but he was gone. I would never get to see Lemmy again. I watched him age every day rapidly on videos. He was withering into a very old man, and I couldn't help but cry. I hated seeing age take him down, because he was Lemmy Kilmister and no one believed that anyone or anything could take him down. Lemmy died December 28, 2015. Our legend was no more. I said it when we lost Randy Rhoads. I said it when we lost Darrell Abbott. It was the day the music died. But the day Lemmy died was truly the day the music died. Our Lemmy. My Lemmy. He was gone. I wanted another chance to tell him again how much he meant to me, but I wouldn't get that chance.

I hope that Lemmy is looking down from heaven to see all of the honors dedicated to him with memorials, testimonials, and monuments being erected. I hope that he can see how many people really, really loved him.

* * *

RIP
Lemmy Kilmister
Born December 25, 1945
Died December 28, 2015

Fly On, Thunderbird

Quiet Riot

I knew about Quiet Riot because of Randy Rhoads, who was one of the original members. But in the '80s there wasn't any way that you couldn't know who Quiet Riot was. They had a number one hit called "Metal Health (Bang Your Head)" that stayed on the charts for what seemed like forever. You couldn't turn on the radio without hearing Quiet Riot. We were really lucky to be on the ride from the beginning. Their manager, John, was the nicest man and so approachable, so we used this opportunity. Debbie and I had been working extra hard on our little magazine *On the Road*, and since Quiet Riot was so hot at the time, we knew we had to spotlight them in our first issue. I always had an instinct about bands, and I felt that they were going to be really big. John had set up a phone interview for me to talk to Kevin DuBrow. Quiet Riot was in Beaumont, Texas, and John gave me Kevin's room number and told me to give him a call, that he'd be expecting it. We introduced ourselves, and then I explained to him that I was extremely nervous. Kevin assured me that there was nothing to be nervous about. We talked about how Quiet Riot got back together the second time around, when Rudy rejoined after leaving Ozzy Osbourne's band. Kevin told me that after Randy Rhoads and Rudy Sarzo left Quiet Riot in 1979 to join Ozzy Osbourne, they changed the name to DuBrow and went on to play the club circuit for two years. They were spotted and signed as DuBrow, but then when Rudy Sarzo left Ozzy Osbourne's band and came back to DuBrow, they changed the name back to Quiet Riot because they all thought it sounded better commercially. I also asked Kevin why Rudy left Ozzy Osbourne's band after Randy Rhoads's death, and he was hesitant about answering questions, since Randy had been in Quiet Riot and they were very good friends. But he said that Rudy felt that the magic was gone after Randy was gone. I said that Randy had really touched so many. We talked about their releases, and I had heard there were two Japanese releases. He told me he had some copies at his house but said he didn't really listen to them because they weren't that good. I'd like to make that judgment. "Metal Health" was getting heavy rotation in the Dallas/Fort Worth area, and he was flattered to hear this. We talked a bit about heavy metal music and how fantastic it was that metal was taking a stand. I asked Kevin about their music and what they considered it to be, and he told me that they didn't like to classify their music and that they just like to get up and play it. Kevin DuBrow was the nicest man, and he really took away my nervousness in the first few minutes of our conversation.

I couldn't wait to see the show. Never had I witnessed a concert such as this one. The show consisted of so much sexual energy and enthusiasm from the Dallas/Fort Worth audience. It was one of those things where you had to be there and experience it yourself. The Bronco Bowl is not a huge arena, possibly holding about 3,500, but this audience got as loud as 20,000 people at Reunion Arena. Near the end of this show, the people got so crazy that they tore all the cushions off the seats and started throwing them, making it look like some sort of Frisbee tournament. I felt that it was partly because Kevin DuBrow had that sort of charisma that turned people on. I know for a fact it turned ladies on, because more than a few ladies left the arena braless and pantieless. Why? Because they were hanging on Mr. DuBrow's mike stand. Kevin was most definitely the source of energy of the group. "They've been tellin' me that I'm getting too nasty. That I've got to clean my act up." A fact, but great. Rudy Sarzo stalked the stage with his bass in the most animalistic manner. He was the ultimate showman, and at one point in the show, he lay on his stomach and proceeded to play the bass that way. Carlos Cavazo screamed on guitar, but it was awfully loud. The highlight of the show was when the drummer, Frankie Banali, rose up from the drum set with the "Metal Health" mask on. The audience went mad!!! All through the show I anticipated one song...with the hope they would play it. I knew when I heard the first chord that it was the song..."Thunderbird." The only time in the entire concert that Kevin DuBrow's voice slightly cracked was when he looked up into the audience to see a banner being held up by his fans. On it it read, "Fly on, Thunderbird. Randy Rhoads." I couldn't help but think that the band members were playing out their hearts for Randy, and it definitely showed. Once I got backstage and actually met Kevin, I discovered that he was most definitely as dynamic a personality offstage as he was on. It was really nice to meet everyone.

John Sykes

Helix w/ Linda

David Coverdale

Brent Doerner & Linda

Quiet Riot/Whitesnake/Helix
October 21, 1984
Reunion Arena, Dallas, Texas

It had been approximately a year since we had seen Quiet
Riot, and all my predictions about their success were completely correct. They were now headlining at Reunion Arena,
and I couldn't wait to visit with them again. After the show we
stood outside Whitesnake's dressing room because Debbie was
intent on meeting the guitarist John Sykes. The bass player,
Neil Murray, joined Debbie and me, and we stood and talked
for a few minutes until he looked at Debbie and informed
her, "John Sykes is in the tuning room." Debbie smiled, and
then we turned to see their drummer, Cozy Powell. He com-
plimented that our stockings were "very lovely." We walked
into the tuning room and there he was, John Sykes, sitting
there like a prince trapped in his special world of electric guitars. He didn't utter a word as we stood listening to our very
own private session. He gazed at us with a certain curiosity as
he strummed his guitar, playing a song that he heard in the
midst of a romantic dream. He was a dream, sitting in a certain majesty that I hadn't seen before, looking like a fantasy,
but he was real, right in front of us. Their manager walked in
and told us that we needed to leave, but John interjected in an
almost primitive way, "No, the girls stay." We smiled at John,
and since we were trying to get in good with the management,
we decided to head to the party in the hospitality room. But

before we left, John told Debbie to meet up with him later backstage.

We ran into Rudy Sarzo, and he asked us where we were going to party. We told him probably Matley's, which was a local Dallas club where a lot of bands went to party after the shows. He hinted that they were partying at the Holiday Inn. I am not sure why, but we ended up going to Matley's, which sort of ended up being quite a fiasco in itself. Ricky Lynn Gregg was playing there that night. He joined us almost immediately telling us we were very beautiful and that we needed drinks. He paid for all our drinks and even went behind the bar to get us a shot himself. But a situation was beginning to build, and we were supposed to go with the guy that owned Matley's and another guy to the Hyatt Regency to meet up with the promoters from 462 Productions. Of course, it didn't take long for us to figure out that we *were* the party, so we decided to head back to Matley's so Lenise could get her car. When I told you it was a fiasco, I meant it. Lenise had locked her keys in the car, so we ended up sleeping on pool tables in the bar until 5:00 a.m. the next morning, when we could finally call a locksmith to come and help us. We finally made it home, totally exhausted.

Road Trip

October 28, 1984
Amarillo Civic Center
Amarillo, Texas

Since the manager told us he would give us tickets and backstage passes if we would follow them to the Amarillo show, Debbie and I decided to go on our first long-distance road trip. We had one hundred dollars and a full tank of gas. We loaded up my little car and left on our trek on what was the longest drive on a never-ending highway to Amarillo, Texas. The gas stations were so far apart—it was really desolate and a little bit frightening, but we were too excited and stupid to be scared of anything. Once we arrived, we immediately checked ourselves into a small motel very close to the arena. The next day we got up and went to the arena to check out the situation and the area, but it didn't seem too complicated, and we figured everything should be just fine. We went back to the motel and slept until showtime, then headed back to the arena. We had VIP backstage passes, of course. Once backstage we sat, drank tea, and socialized with Neil Murray. Debbie disappeared with Whitesnake's manager, Jimmy. When she returned, we went to watch some of Helix's show; then suddenly our eyes widened to see Rudy Sarzo, in a pair of underwear, and John Sykes running across the stage, throwing pies at Helix. At first I didn't know what the hell was happening, but I quickly learned that it was the end-of-the-tour party as well as Kevin DuBrow's birthday, and it was all about fucking with one another while they were onstage. When Helix came offstage, Brent Doerner stopped for pictures with us, and we even got a little lick of the pie that was smashed all over his face. Before Whitesnake went onstage, they stood with us on the side stage. Neil Murray had on a Dallas sweatshirt, and he said he wore it because he knew we'd be here. Once they went onstage, Debbie and I decided to go back to the restroom, where we ran into Brent again, except this time he was smoking a joint with some girls. We just laughed and went about our business. Debbie left to see the Whitesnake show, and I ended up talking with the guys from Helix. They had cameras and video cameras, and they kept taking pictures of me. I hopped up on top of an equipment box, but supposedly I didn't know I shouldn't be sitting on it. Jokingly, they picked me up and put me inside the box for a minute or two, but then of course they let me out. I talked them into doing the same thing to Debbie, so I called her over and they did. It was so funny, and the pictures were great! We made it to the stage for Quiet Riot's show, and we were sitting up onstage to the side. We couldn't wait to see what festivities were going to take place, but we figured it was going to be good. Their drummer, Frankie Banali, was so drunk he fell off the drum set, and their manager, John, had to take over for him. The next thing I remember is Helix was standing backstage dressed in black garbage bags, and Brent looked straight at me and raised his bag up a little bit, revealing his nakedness. I waved and smiled at him. They ran onstage dancing a cute little jig, then first mooning Quiet Riot, then mooning the unsuspecting audience. It was not Whitesnake's turn, but with their class, they had hired a lady to go out onto the stage and strip down to her panties for Kevin. Amarillo, Texas, really got a great show that night, unaware of all the festivities that took place. What a treat!

Backstage, David Coverdale thanked us for coming all the way from Dallas to see them again. He leaned down, kissed my lips, and then gently bit my lip. My heart was racing so fast. He smelled so good, like a real man should smell. After the show and all the festivities were over, we headed over to the Holiday Inn to party with Quiet Riot. The security was very tight, but Carlos Cavazo managed to push me up and down the hallways while riding a nightstand that had wheels. We hung out in the sauna and the swimming pool. There were a few local girls (not really groupies) that were hanging around us, and they said they didn't know you could have so much fun and thanked us. You gotta train them, right? If you are going to hang around with rock bands, you gotta know how to party like them too.

Debbie and I had so much fun, but we knew we had to head back to Arlington, Texas, so we hit the road. It was an experience that we would never forget.

We would lose Kevin DuBrow in 2007 to a drug overdose. Kevin had a lot of demons, and losing his very best friend, Randy Rhoads, weighed hard on him, and I don't think he ever got over it. Randy had that effect on a lot of people. Kevin was a very nice man, and I was honored to be able to spend as much time as I did with him.

* * *

We lost Frankie Banali as well.
RIP
Born November 14, 1951
Died August 20, 2020

We also lost Cozy Powell.
RIP
Born December 29, 1947
Died April 5, 1998

Scream for Me, Dallas!

February 27, 1985
at the Arcadia Theater in Dallas, Texas

February 28, 1985
at Cardi's Theater in Houston, Texas

April 4, 1986
at Reunion Arena in Dallas, Texas

We had massively gotten into metal music. The glam scene was kind of falling to the wayside, and the rage of heavy metal was taking over. There was a new band called Metallica that was coming on strong and was not to be ignored. We knew we had to experience them before they became untouchable. They were scheduled to play February 27, 1985 at the Arcadia Theater with Armored Saint as the opening act. This chick we knew was with us, and she had brought an ample amount of drugs for us to use, as well as to share with the band. We were doing cocaine and speed mixed in this little tubelike contraption called a bullet, and you would place it in your nostril, then pull back the trigger and shoot it. It was a trip! The band liked us so much they begged us to go to Houston, Texas, and after talking it over, we decided that we would fly on our own so we could come home when we wanted to. There was one problem with that: I had never flown before, and I was terrified. That chick we knew had a lot of money, and Southwest Airlines was having a deal where you flew and your friend flew free, so it wasn't too bad. I desperately tried to talk myself out of it but someone called Cliff and told him I was chickening out, and he was frantic, telling them to load me up on drinks and get me on that plane no matter what. They did what he requested and proceeded to get me thoroughly drunk and on that plane, and I am proud to say that I did it. During this time there weren't many men that could outdrink us. There was a bar called Savvy's in Fort Worth, and it ran a drink special where it was five dollars for a tray filled with shots. This chick we knew would order a stack of five trays, and when that was empty, more would always come. It was absolutely blithering excess.

By the time we arrived in Houston, Texas, I was well drunk. We took a taxi to the hotel for our reunion with the band, but short as it was, we switched over to a limousine and headed to Cardi's, where they were playing that night. Cliff and I were lip-locked the whole way there, unable to keep our hands off of each other. I don't know what the deal was between Cliff and me, but there was an enormous, passionate, and sexual connection between the two of us. I honestly hadn't experienced this sort of connection with anyone. During the show we were standing up on some type of platform that stood higher than the audience, and the band could see us perfectly. At one point James went to the microphone and sang out, "Scream for me, Dallas!!!" We were screaming, jumping up and down. It was an incredible moment! After the show we stood outside the tour buses waiting for the band to join us again. The guys in Armored Saint were standing inside their tour bus smiling and making gestures toward us. We were not in any way reciprocating the behavior; however, Cliff perceived it differently. He took my arm and abruptly led me over to the bus and directly to the back room. He shut the door; then he quickly turned back around with his hand up, striking me across the face so hard that I fell backward onto the small table. I lay completely still for a second and then slowly started to rise up, scared to death because I had never been hit by a man. Cliff blurted out, "Why were you flirting with the other band?? You are mine!!"

He laid his hand gently against my face while I said, "I wasn't. They were trying to flirt with us." He pulled me into his arms, apologizing over and over, telling me he just overreacted and didn't mean to do it. I just agreed and then pleaded to go back into the front of the bus with my friends. Needless to say, they were not happy to hear what had just happened, and I thought Debbie was going to get up and kill him, but I calmed her down.

I was nervous for the first time being alone with him after he hit me, and I didn't know what to expect. With the addition of more drinking, all the animalistic passions came back, and everything was fine from that point on. The next morning Cliff begged me to go on the tour with him, but I couldn't leave my friends behind; besides, I had a small distrust in him. Cliff told me Debbie had slept in Kirk's room because Kirk had not been in it all night. He explained that Lenise was in the room next to Kirk's when we needed her. He pulled me over to the window. "If you stand here, I will be able to look up and see you to wave goodbye." He kissed me goodbye and left. I went to the window and watched for Cliff, and when he got on the sidewalk by the bus, he waved up to me, and I waved back. After a few seconds, Cliff began pointing and waving more heartily. I was confused, waving back. But then Cliff began calling all the other band members over, the roadies and even the fucking bus driver. Okay, this is a bit extreme, Cliff, I thought while I stupidly waved to everyone. We all gathered back together and left for the airport.

On the way home I began talking to people on the plane. The man next to me just happened to be the tour manager for Iron Maiden, and you guessed it! We were completely set up for tickets and backstage passes for the Dallas show. I was so happy to get back home to our apartment and rest. Cliff immediately started calling, and he was laughing, wanting to explain to me about what happened back in Houston when he was waving up at me. He said that Lenise was standing by the window naked while smoking a cigarette and she didn't know that everyone on the sidewalk could look up and see her. I started laughing, and I couldn't wait to tell Lenise. Cliff also kept begging me to come to El Paso for their shows, but we just couldn't come up with the money. I was just feeling so tired and not feeling very well. I sort of wanted to go home for some Mom-and-Dad time. I ended up staying for a few days, and while I was there, Cliff called, and my dad answered the telephone. Dad kept looking at me oddly; then he finally handed me the phone, saying, "It's some bass player." I couldn't help but laugh. I talked to Cliff for a while, and then I let him go. I didn't know it at the time, but when I met Cliff again, he would be a completely different person.

I wouldn't see Cliff again until May 10, 1986, at the Tarrant County Convention Center, when Metallica was opening up for Ozzy Osbourne. Everyone had changed. They were all arrogant, even Cliff, who was always so down to earth. He tried to be with me, but I didn't feel the same. I didn't have the same attraction for Cliff as I did before. I wasn't the same, and I felt my life was on the precipice of major changes.

Cliff and I talked on the telephone several times, but eventually that stopped. During this period of time, a lot of things had transpired, and I ended up moving home to start making positive changes in my life.

Late in September, I received a telephone call from one of my friends asking if I had heard the news.

"What news?"

Metallica was touring in Sweden and was involved in a major accident, and Cliff Burton was killed. My stomach dropped as I hung up the telephone. I was literally in shock. Cliff was only twenty-four years old.

I had received a letter from a friend named Damon, and in the letter he wrote, "Cliff Burton was fucking nuts about you." I smiled, thinking to myself, "Yeah, he was."

* * *

RIP
Cliff Burton
Born February 10, 1962
Died September 27, 1986

Linda & Debbie

Prince Charming

Black 'N Blue

Aerosmith/Black 'N Blue/Stone Fury
December 13, 1984

KISS/Black 'N Blue
December 4, 1985

Yngwie Malmsteen/Lita Ford/Black 'N Blue
June 3, 1988

Every now and then, Debbie and I would get tidbits of information that would help us on whatever quests we were on at the time, and this time we were on the search for the new up-and-coming Black 'N Blue. A product of John Kalodner from Geffen Records and produced by Gene Simmons of KISS, they were churning out hit after hit, such as "Hold On to 18." There was the special added attraction that they were absolutely gorgeous in Debbie's and my book—they checked every corner of the square. Our tipster informed us that the guys in Black 'N Blue were staying overnight in Dallas, Texas, so we did what groupies do…We headed out, scoping the area, and we figured out they were staying at a local hotel we were quite familiar with. We started off at the hotel bar, where we met a dude named Ziggy who confirmed that the two bands were staying there. We looked up to see Stone Fury leave down the elevator, so we decided to follow suit, and when we got down to the lobby, Black 'N Blue stepped out of the elevator, saw us, and called out, "GIRLS!" They clamored around us, explaining that they were going to a club called the Ritz and wanted us to go with them, so we piled into a van. The lead singer, Jaime St. James, drove while I gave him the directions on how to get there. An awesome drummer named Randy Castillo was also with us for the ride. Once at the bar, Debbie and I walked in on guitarist Tommy Thayer's arms, and he whispered to us, "I have to maintain my rock star image." Tommy was special, and you could just tell that he had a special star quality about him, and I just knew that it was going to take him very far.

The guys sort of spread out all over the bar, playing video games, pool, and the like, but Debbie and I did what we did best: dancing flirty on the dance floor. "Jailbreak" began playing, and while we danced, we hadn't noticed that one of our closest friends had sneaked up onto the dance floor with us. It was Casey Orr of Rigor Mortis and later Gwar fame, and he stood in between Debbie and me with his arms crossed and wearing a tough, stoic face. We didn't let him bother us at all, and we just continued to flirt suggestively around him. Patrick walked over to the side of the stage, took my hand, and helped me down from the dance floor. "Did he embarrass you?"

I smiled at him. "No, not at all."

When Led Zeppelin came over the speaker system, Jamie said, "That's before our time!" And with that we piled back into the van—around Tommy, of course. Jamie did a handstand in the front seat, and then we headed to the hotel. Instead of staying the night, we kissed and said our goodbyes till the next night.

The next night, we found out they got us front-row center seats and backstage passes. It was a great show, and they saw us and smiled down at us. After the show we stood backstage talking with all the guys. They decided to go to a party at a club called Trax and wanted us to go with them. We found ourselves sitting alone at first, but Patrick came over, bringing me a drink. He said, "I was beginning to worry about Miss Lonely." He smiled so sweetly at me, and I was definitely feeling it. Jamie came over, continuing to pour us drinks and heavily flirting with Debbie. Patrick would lean over to me doing Cowardly Lion impressions. He was absolutely precious, and I adored him. He missed his calling—he would have made the perfect Prince Charming.

The next time I saw Black 'N Blue was December 4, 1985, with KISS. It was a great show, but the highlight was being with the band at the end of the night.

The last time I would see Black 'N Blue was June 3, 1988, with Yngwie Malmsteen and Lita Ford. Debbie and I went together, but things didn't go as I wanted them to. Patrick was very distant, and I figured he was being faithful to someone. I might have been a little hurt and disappointed, but I seriously respected him for it. Debbie managed to get backstage, but because I wouldn't suck a little dick, I didn't. It wasn't a big deal. My car was parked backstage, so I just hopped on my hood and settled in. The funniest thing happened when I looked up to see Lita Ford walking over to me because her manager had told her that I wouldn't suck dick for a backstage pass. She smiled and me said, "Why wouldn't you suck a dick for a backstage pass?"

I looked straight at her face and said, "Nah, I never wanted in a show bad enough to suck a stranger's dick."

Lita smiled, looked over to her manager, and said, "Get this girl a backstage pass!"

I met up with Debbie backstage, and we watched the shows, and afterward we went back to the hotel to hang out with the band. Even though things had changed so much, I felt lucky to have this last moment with them.

Patrick Young & Linda

We Were Scammed!

Billy Squier
November 11, 1988, Bronco Bowl

One of my long-term road-crew friends set me up with backstage passes and tickets for the Billy Squier concert. No one was available to go, so I decided to ask my brother Terry to the show. I had never taken my brother to a concert before, and only God knows how long it had been since Terry had been to a concert, and he was in for the shock of his life. I tried to explain to him what was likely in store for him, but he assured me that he had been around, seen and done things I couldn't even fathom. Okay, big bro, I thought—we'll see. We were sitting in some really decent balcony seats at the Bronco Bowl—we were even with the stage, and the groupies were gathering around us, letting me know these were the seats allotted for the band's guests. There were three groupies that I think knew something was up with my brother, because he definitely had the look of not exactly fitting in, so they decided to put on a little show for him, dancing all about in front of him. Not that big of a deal, right? Did I mention that their tits were partially hanging out and they had on miniskirts without panties? I couldn't help but smile, but believe it or not, he seemed to be handling the situation as well as any man would. Finally it was time to go backstage, and once we were backstage, the festivities continued. The groupies started in again, dancing around flirtingly right in Terry's view, every so often bending over so Terry could get a full view of everything very clearly. I'll swear, his eyes were so wide I was afraid they would fall right out of his head. I think he finally understood what I was talking about when I warned him about the backstage area.

But believe it or not, the best was yet to come. Billy Squier's guitarist, Jimmy Crespo, and his lovely wife came over to chat with us and finally invited us to come with them onto the tour bus so we could get to know one other better. We agreed, accepting their invitation, and accompanied them out to the tour bus. They provided us drinks and sat back, enjoying our company. Jimmy Crespo pulled me to the side to talk mostly with him, while Jimmy Crespo's wife did the same with Terry. I sort of thought it was fishy, and then it began to take that awkward turn, and all warning alerts went off. We were being scammed! Wait! I was not used to being the one being scammed—I was usually the one to do the scamming. They wanted to have sex with us, like an orgy switch-up. *Ew!* I said, "No! No! No! Terry is my brother!"

Jimmy's wife smiled. "That doesn't matter."

I stood up. "Terry, we need to go now." Terry looked bewildered and did not know what was going on. I reached down and grabbed his arm and said more sternly. "Terry, we need to go!" I turned to Jimmy Crespo and his wife and thanked them and said our goodbyes.

I was practically dragging Terry out of there, and while we walked to my car, I began explaining to him what exactly was going on. Terry stopped and stared at me in shock. "WHAT? No way! Really?"

Nodding my head, I said, "Um yeah, that is what was happening."

"Oh shit!"

Terry and I started laughing. We got into my car and drove away from a very strange situation. I won't forget it, and I doubt very seriously that Terry will ever forget it.

Beautiful Boys

Bret Michaels—Poison
October 23, 1985
December 14, 1986
May 7, 1988

I am not sure how I learned about Poison, but I don't doubt I was gazing at the album *Look What the Cat Dragged In* and thinking, "Holy shit! These are the most beautiful guys I have ever seen!"

Okay, so they wore more makeup than I did, used more hairspray than I did, and even had better clothes than I did. I had to meet them! I had been hanging around with a dancer friend of mine by the name of Ramie, so I asked her if she would accompany me, and she said yes. I thought she would make a great scammer, but the only problem was she was very beautiful, with a spot-on perfect body. I didn't have a chance, but it was still worth the fun. We knew Poison was playing at the Ritz so we headed that way, and after flirting around a bit, one of the roadies told us they were staying at the motel behind the Ritz, so that is where we headed. It was really pretty funny, because we pulled up in this little motor court, and one of the motel-room doors opened up, and a bunch of pretty boys stuck their heads out. "GIRLS!" they screamed out like little boys on Christmas morning. "Come on over!" they called out. We popped back into the car and pulled it over into a parking spot, then joined them in the motel room. It was rather cute because they acted just like young boys, so excited. It didn't take long for us to start talking and enjoying one another's company. I was sitting on the dresser and put on Bret's military hat, and I posed flirtingly for photographs. Bret grabbed his acoustic guitar and sat down right beside me, starting to play and sing to me. It was so beautiful. The attention I was getting was quickly diverted when Ramie agreed to take her shirt off to show them her titties, let them touch them and take pictures with them. Granted, her titties were very beautiful, but that was something I would have never done, even with all of my groupie experience. Sucks to be so shy, because my tits are really the bomb! Trust me, Ian Gillan from Deep Purple told me so. They set us up to get in free for the show, but they didn't have backstage passes because their first tour was extremely low budget. During the show, they spent a lot of their time staring at us. Once the show was over, everything just kind of stopped. I knew where Bret was, and he was with Ramie. She assured me before the show that she would be with Bret. I left and went home.

Almost one year had gone by, and Poison's career skyrocketed to the top. You couldn't turn on MTV without a Poison video on the screen. It was really something, but I had pretty much put my experience with Poison in the past and just didn't think about it much. Then on December 14, 1986, I received a phone call from Poison's manager, and he told me to come to the Hard Rock Cafe in Dallas, Texas, for a surprise. I was really rather confused about what was going on. Once we arrived, we were escorted upstairs to the private VIP lounge, and once up there I was most definitely surprised. It was a party with so many beautiful people, and one of those people standing there with a big beautiful smile was Bret Michaels. We hugged and kissed. Fame had definitely agreed with him, and he looked wonderful. I looked around at all the beautiful people drinking and having a wonderful time, and my eyes widened as I saw Weird Al Yankovic walking up with two beautiful girls on each arm. He was very friendly and funny. I was having such a good time getting to know everyone and taking pictures. I was standing by myself when I was approached by the Cult's Ian Astbury, and he was drunk and in a sloppy way started putting the moves on me. I thought he was incredibly rude and immediately completely disliked him. He got angry that I was not accepting his advances, and he told me he was going to have me removed from the party, and it just so happened that Bret stepped up and said, "You can't throw her out because she is my guest." Bret smiled at me and led me away toward the bar, where we snapped some pictures together. It was a lovely time, and I enjoyed the moment very much.

I wouldn't see them again until May 7, 1988, at Reunion Arena. The show was great! After the show, even better. I was the last girl on the bus while everyone else was asked to leave. So much fun with the guys. They were standing only in towels at the door of the tour bus, which was guarded by a very large security guard. I was able to watch them sign autographs for all the screaming girls, and I snapped a great picture.

But the whole reason I wrote this chapter about Poison is for my friendship with Bret Michaels, the guys in Poison, and also their amazing management. Extraordinary moments happen, and this particular incident claims a spot at the very top of the list.

It had been well over thirty years, and I had long since retired my groupie boots. I was a wife and a mother of two children and working as a head cashier at a local grocery store. I am a very friendly person, and I would say it's an under-statement to say I know everyone and everyone knows me. That being said, you can get to know people on a personal level, and that is where this story technically begins. This lady would come into the store shopping, bringing with her Violet, her four-year-old daughter. Violet was the most beautiful little spitfire you could ever meet, and so very personable. She won me over the first time I ever met her, and it didn't take very long for me to learn the most important thing about her: she was madly in love with Poison's lead singer, Bret Michaels. Her mother explained how she liked to dress up just like him with the bandana, leather, and eyeliner. She knew all his songs. It really was the cutest thing you ever saw.

I saw it coming at a hundred miles per hour like a Mack truck in my rearview mirror, and one day her mom came into the store and straight to me. "I know you knew Bret back in the day. He's playing Billy Bob's Texas in Fort Worth. Can you set it up so my baby can meet him?" Yeah, that was pretty much what I thought was gonna happen. I was panicked, to say the least, to be put in such a position. It had been so long ago, over thirty years, so how in the world could I possibly pull this off?

It's a long story, and I won't get totally into it until a later chapter, but my daughter got me involved in booking bands, so I had developed a lot of great contacts. One of those contacts was Bret's manager and a musician himself, Pete Evick. I honestly didn't want to put any stock into Bret remembering me. Pete was my only chance, so I messaged him over the internet explaining the whole story to him. He told me he would approach Bret and ask. Shockingly, Bret remembered me and agreed to meet Violet, so Pete set it all up. To say I was flabbergasted doesn't even come close to covering how I felt.

So Violet, accompanied by her very protective daddy, went to see the Bret Michaels concert at Billy Bob's Texas. When you are only four years old, having to wait till after a concert is over, especially when your bedtime is normally at 8:00 p.m., is excruciating. Violet did a lot of napping on her daddy's shoulder until the meet and greet. She was super excited, her and her daddy singing all the songs together. After the show, Violet was moved to the front of the line at the meet and greet. She was really nervous, not knowing what to say, so her daddy helped out with the conversation. They took several pictures. Bret was a superstar and absolutely made this little girl's dreams come true. I came out of the whole story pretty high up on the ladder myself. Violet's mother told me that about a month later, a friend of theirs was working on the stage set up at another one of Bret's shows, and when the friend told Bret that he knew little Violet, Bret gave a guitar pick and a signed guitar strap for her.

So after all the excitement and events happened, Pete called me, telling me Bret wanted to make sure that I was happy with him after everything he did, and of course I laughed and said yes. Bret, I'll never forget what you did to make that little girl's dreams come true. Thank you!

Linda w/ Bret Michaels

Bret Michaels w/ Linda

Bret Michaels & Rikki Rocket
signing autographs

Linda in
Bret Michaels' hat

Bret Michaels

So You Wanna Be a Groupie?

"Why did you want to be a groupie?" people ask me. "I mean, did you just wake up one day and say, 'I think I might be a groupie when I grow up'?"

Oh hell, I don't know how to explain it. It's complicated to say the least. I was definitely raised right, taught all the essential morals and values. Other than my being overly smothered and protected, there wasn't anything out of the ordinary about me except maybe my being molested when I was a little girl. Unfortunately I can't analyze myself to tell you whether or not it made me a loose woman or not because I never completed my psychology degree. Plus I was a virgin until I was twenty-one years old, so that doesn't necessarily scream out "I'm a slut!" What I can tell you is that growing up was very difficult for me. I was constantly ridiculed at school, never accepted by "the norm" or the cliques, and shunned for being different. It made it easy for me to slip off into my world of make-believe and daydreams. I was just an insecure teenager with very little confidence, so I would seek out acceptance in the arms of the very people I dreamed about, approval to make me feel worthwhile and special. It was a tightrope stretched across two worlds, and I lost my balance falling into it, and there was no turning back.

"Groupie" isn't a bad word. There have always been girls (and guys) who wholeheartedly followed the people they dreamed about and eventually strive to be with, whether these were musicians, actors, sports figures, or even military personnel. When I was growing up, we lived near a military air force base, and when I was in high school, there was a group of girls who fantasized about meeting or marrying a "fly boy." They would hang out at the bars outside the base and do whatever it took. In fact, throughout history there have always been groupies. Pan from Greek mythology had the nymphs as his groupies. In all my research, I think the oddest example of groupies was the women who followed the men who pursued the path of penance through flagellation by flogging themselves throughout the streets. That is some crazy shit!

So why rock stars? I have always had a connection to music one way or another. My brothers were both heavily into music, especially Terry, so they were probably my first real influence. My mother was very supportive of my interest in music, buying me albums and rock magazines. I loved listening to their old albums from Elvis Presley and Petula Clark, as well as loads of old country and bluegrass. My dad and his family were all musically gifted and would gather every week on the grandparents' front porch to play music. Unfortunately I didn't get any of that musical talent. Mom took me for piano lessons, but it wasn't piano I learned about. The piano teacher was having an extramarital affair while she was supposed to teach me how to play the piano. I could play the hell out of scales on top of learning all about the thralls of sexual passion. Mom would pick me up afterward and ask if I learned anything good. I would grin and say, "Oh yeah, I sure did." My musical interests started off innocently enough with "Puppy Love" by

Donny Osmond, the Jackson Five, and of course the Bay City Rollers. Innocent enough, right? Just a teenager idolizing the bands as if they were some type of deities. At that time in my life, I wasn't even thinking about them as in sexual relations, forming intricate or meaningful relationships. I can most surely blame Aerosmith for that little honor. I had this titillating pull-out poster that, once it was pulled out, had a couple of secret flaps to fold out. It revealed Steven Tyler with his arms crossed across his chest, a small red vest, and blue jeans that were unbuttoned and unzipped to show black luscious tufts of pubic hair, probably way too much for that day and time. I don't know how they got away with that, but I'm glad they did. I could, and I did, sit and stare at that poster for hours, getting all sorts of tingles in my nether regions. Woo! My mom even saw it: "That's vulgar!" Shockingly, she didn't make me get rid of it but instead made me fold it up out of view.

It wasn't until I met Debbie that I realized that we had the capabilities to make all our dreams and fantasies a reality. Oh, that feeling…It's the one I find so difficult to write into words. I reflect on that insecure teenager just trying to find acceptance, and not only was I accepted, but I was a part of that world. I was standing backstage with a VIP backstage pass hanging around my neck. I was watching the rock star performing in front of twenty thousand or more fans, and he was the object of every girl's desire, and I realized that he had chosen me! At last I had the validation I had sought after as a young girl, that feeling of importance and being desired. I would be the only one to accompany him back to the hotel.

If you were a groupie, for however long you had, you would give him everything he wanted or needed, whether it be sexual gratification, just talking, or maybe just lying down and holding him close to you through the night.

The most important part of being a groupie is to be a very strong individual mentally. These guys come into town and engulf your life for one or two days, longer if you are lucky, but whatever the circumstances are, it makes it very hard to let go and walk away. If you are one of the lucky ones, he will remember you year after year. Probably the most intriguing story from the '70s was about the beautiful Audrey Hamilton, who lived in Dallas, Texas. She met the "Golden God," Robert Plant from Led Zeppelin. It seems she was a very lucky and very special groupie who was able to lasso his heart, captivating him enough that he took her on the entire tour with him, which is a very unusual event to happen.

You have to practically brainwash your mind and your heart that down the line there will be another town and another girl that he will treat just as well as he treated you. Not everyone can be as lucky as Audrey. Me? I seemed to pair up with the genuine dudes who would want to see me every time they came to town. And I am also still in touch with them today. For instance, I have been friends with John Gallagher from the metal group Raven for well over thirty years. He even helped my son with a college project, spending over an hour on the telephone with him. My son scored 110 percent on that project. But John is a very important person to me and always will be. But you always need to protect yourself because some rock stars can be really disrespectful and treat groupies like a piece of shit and have no regard for their feelings. Boy, could I ever make you a list.

Just like Audrey Hamilton, there have been legends that came before us who were classics, and I always pay homage to them. There was Cynthia Plaster Caster, who had the greatest gimmick ever, making plaster casts of rock star dongs. Grand Funk Railroad immortalized "Sweet Connie" in the infamous hit "American Band." I had the distinct pleasure of meeting her backstage once, and she told me I looked like Stevie Nicks. And no one can forget the incomparable Pamela Des Barres, who became a best-selling author, writing about all her escapades, and who married rock star royalty and actor Michael Des Barres. Groupies have come before us, and they will surely come after us.

Every era will have its own groupies, and in each there will be distinct differences that make each unique in its own right. In the '60s and '70s, it was all about peace, love, and drugs. You had so many bands coming onto the scene—the accessibility must have been easier, and there was just a newness that made everything so exciting. The '80s brought to us the big-budget touring, filling huge arenas, and bands who were unusually more beautiful than the groupies or female fans. In the '90s metal and grunge began moving onto the scene, bringing about scaled down-touring, festival shows, and smaller budgets. I had to confer with Debbie a lot when it came to the '90s and 2000s, when I was very busy being married and making babies. She says these later decades brought about the ability to use "the internet and social media, which created a gazillion more ways for fans to connect with artists and vice versa." She went on to explain that "in the 2000s most of the legwork for those hookups was done online, via emails."

So who knows what the future will bring to the world of music and groupies? Will we even be a part of the process with artificial intelligence taking over?

Debbie and I made our groupie experiences an art, creating a guidebook, a little one-two-three how-to. But remember this was during the 1980s, so keep in mind that each era will be different from the next.

While it is universally believed that musicians are in it only for the hot chicks and getting laid, honestly that couldn't be further from the truth. I have spoken with so many musicians, and the consensus for why they wanted to become musicians was their love of and creation of music. Along the same lines, I asked the many musicians about groupies and what made some groupies stand out differently from the others, and the answer was for them to understand and actually love the music. Debbie's long-term boyfriend, named Michael, explained, "[What] strikes me as being so different about groupies in this age range and younger is they know nothing about music and don't really care to know. And that is a huge turnoff." Debbie added, "He's not alone in that regard because at the end of the day, sex or not, it's still about that human connection. And having common interests gives you something to talk about before, during, and after sex. Learn as much as you can about the music and love it with real sincerity, and the rest will work itself out."

So the most important things a wannabe groupie needs to do are…

Engulf yourself in the music!

Support the bands any way possible, such as by starting a fan club.

Contact the record company representatives and start promotions. They are more than willing to send you posters, stickers, and demos, and by helping out you just might score yourself some complimentary tickets for your help. My daughter helped support the bands she loved through Warner Brothers Records.

Remember this little tip: Always support your local bands because they just might be the next up-and-coming hitmakers.

Be patient with yourself. In the beginning Debbie and I were so naive and didn't know anything about the backstage world, but we were anxious to learn, so we watched the other groupies, and it didn't take long for us to figure it all out. Our very first experience lit a fire inside us that could not be extinguished. Once we were backstage, it was as if we turned into someone else, and it consumed us.

Okay, so now you want to get that backstage pass. Who should you get it from? You've got a lot of options to choose from, but you have to be very careful with choices because they may reflect how people view you, and trust me—even though you would think the backstage area is huge, it isn't. Everyone knows everything. For instance, we were backstage with Krokus, and this girl had been following the band for weeks. She had been sucking dick and fucking roadies to get in at all the shows, and word had gotten back to the band. We were talking with the guitarist Fernando Von Arb, and he pointed her out to us. "See her? She is our latest walking herpes display." Ouch!

So if you give yourself a bad reputation, it can be really hard to shake. Let me throw a little advice out there. Bands do not want to be with the groupie who has spread it all around to everyone. I always reflect on the "Young Lust" scene from Pink Floyd's *The Wall*, where the groupies are walking down the ramp then proceed to do the security guards and then the roadies, all for that laminated pass.

A lot of different people carry backstage passes. Promoters of the concert. The manager of the band. The tour manager. The roadies. The band.

Promoters are usually pretty decent guys, and it's entirely possible to get in tight with one of them, and then the promoter will be more than happy to give you a backstage pass. Make a good impression, and remember, these guys are extremely busy and under a lot of pressure. This was Debbie's and my preferred method of getting our backstage passes. We were really good friends with several of the promoters. They were more than happy to have pretty and classy girls backstage.

Managers can go in both directions. Some believe that if they give you a backstage pass, expectations must be met. But some managers can be great connections. I have known some really decent managers who never expected anything from me and also got me into a lot of extra concerts that I normally would not have attended.

Roadies are the hardest-working dudes in the business, and most are salt of the earth; however, most are complete scumbags who will take advantage of you with little to no remorse. Let me explain to you a phrase that is widely used by roadies: "code of the road." This phrase basically means if you are a girl wanting to get a backstage pass, you must pay the price by giving head to and/or having sex with a roadie. If you resort to this method, then your backstage pass will have a code letter that will let everyone, including the band, know how you got your backstage pass. Tricky, huh? Debbie and I learned this little tidbit of information from a band we knew, so we never did anything with a roadie for a backstage pass. It was too risky for getting a bad reputation there; we were known as "the girls who didn't earn their passes." That was fine with me, and I wore that badge proudly. I did have roadies who were friends and respected me for my choices. I used to hang out with Paul Stanley's guitar technician. His tour name was Romeo because he looked a lot like Paul, so he was gorgeous, and we continued to see each other every year.

Drugs! Did you read the chapter I wrote regarding drugs? Don't do drugs, *fool*! Drugs are bad!! Debbie and I never used this method, but a lot of groupies do use drugs to get in with the bands and to get backstage passes. I have so many funny stories dealing with drugs and being backstage. I remember I was hanging out with some roadies who were friends of mine, doing cocaine in their tour bus. Suddenly, Dave Mustaine from Megadeth opened the door and walked in, and his eyes went straight to me. "My cocaine is better. Come with me!"

He grabbed my hand, leading me out of the bus among the groans of my roadie friends. Another time Debbie and I were actually with Cheap Trick at their hotel, partying. Someone began passing a huge joint around for everyone to smoke, even the band. It didn't take long for us to realize that the huge joint was mixed with something other than marijuana. We did not like it because we were far too fucked up, which made us have to work too hard to keep it together, plus the guys began talking about chickens or something on a farm. Robin Zander turned to me, asking a question, and I was so stupidly fucked up that my response was simply "Uh...no...I think we gotta go." I grabbed Debbie's hand, and we left. I don't know how we made it home. We were both so embarrassed we acted like that in front of Cheap Trick.

The band is the other option to get a backstage pass, and most of the time that will just be pure luck, being in the right place at the right time. Debbie and I were the poster girls for pure luck.

I have been simply standing in the audience, minding my own business, when I was approached by the band's tour manager holding a backstage pass. He went on to explain that I had been spotted by the band and my presence was requested backstage. That, my friend, is pure luck. Remember that you have a very special power, and that power resides in your eyes. You can believe me or not, but if you know how, you can get a backstage pass simply with eye contact. I used to stand by the barricade and seductively stare up at one of the band members until I knew he was getting turned on, and before you knew it, I had a backstage pass slapped on my shirt. Try it at a bar or restaurant sometime. Pick someone out and stare at the person in a seductive manner, not in a creepy way, and see what happens. You will either get thrown out or get a date for the evening.

While we are on the subject of the band, there are just a couple of things I would like to cover. The tour bus is a status symbol, and making it onto the band's tour bus is a huge accomplishment for a groupie. The tour bus is a person's home away from home, so be observant, because it can tell you a whole lot about who band members are. There is a lot you can learn. For instance, Debbie and I were on the Mötley Crüe tour bus, and before the band came on to join, I had the chance to do a little inspection. First off, the first thing that hit you was the smell. It smelled like a men's locker room, but even more powerful was the smell of sex. It almost made you want to gag. As I walked along, I started looking at the cushions on the chairs and couches, and I couldn't believe what I was seeing. It was sex stains. I couldn't bring myself to touch them because they were palpable sex stains, and if I had touched them, they would have had sticky strings. EW! I started to go in between the personal bunks, and it felt like a brick wall of stank hitting me. I said, turning to Debbie and Lenise, that we should get the hell out of there. We did. Years later I had the chance to party with them yet again at this really nice hotel. Everyone was naked in a hot tub. I reflected on my past experience and couldn't get it out of my head, and no matter what I did, all I could see was a big stewpot of STDs. I left as fast as I could. Also, just a little input—the back room of the bus is a private room *with* a lock. Make sure you don't find yourself trapped in there with someone you don't trust.

Finally, put your detective hat on! Be adventurous! Get the bands' itineraries and figure out where they may have lay-overs. Use your shrewdness and cunning, explore the hotels, and hang out in the hotel bars. Do the legwork! You won't believe all the fun you can have, all the people you can meet, and all the new places you can discover. What do you have to lose when you have so much to gain? Trust me, if you know the right people, the city comes alive at midnight, and you can have one hell of a ride. After I moved home, I talked my mom into allowing me to take her around to all the fantastic hotels and amazing places I had experienced. She had never seen such things except on television, and I think for a split second she understood why that time of my life was so extraordinary and what it meant to me.

Alice Cooper/Guns N' Roses

December 4, 1987
Reunion Arena

Oh my God, I cannot believe that I had concert tickets to see Alice Cooper, who was one of my all-time favorite performers. I didn't care whether or not I received a backstage pass—I was just absolutely thrilled to have the chance to see him live.

Wouldn't you know it, one of the tour managers walked up to my friend and me on the floor of the arena, handing us two backstage passes. "The band has spotted you and wants you to be backstage." We honestly couldn't help but giggle at our luck.

The opening act for Alice Cooper was Guns N' Roses, which was the newest young band on the fast track to superstardom. Their show was really incredible, but I honestly just couldn't wait to see Alice Cooper.

The show started, and it was just as I suspected, absolutely incredible! It was Alice Cooper! My friend and I were standing side by side watching the show when all of a sudden Axl Rose, the lead singer for Guns N' Roses, came bursting in between us, pushing us apart so he was standing in front of us watching the show. I actually lost my temper, shocked at his actions. "Who the FUCK do you think you are?" He ignored me, continuing to watch the show. I would not have been so upset, but where we were standing, there wasn't anyone standing around us, and he could have easily gone around us. Whatever! I wasn't going to let him ruin the Alice Cooper concert for me.

After the show, we went backstage, meeting all the guys from Alice Cooper's band. We unfortunately didn't get to meet Alice Cooper, but we still had the most incredible time. Afterward, we decided to extend the night's festivities by going to a local nightclub by the name of Matley's in Dallas, Texas. We were standing along the wall when all of a sudden there was a disturbance coming from the rear of the club. I was trying to figure out what was going on when I saw Axl Rose walking out of the crowd of clambering people, and he walked the walkway where we were standing and stopped in front of me with a huge grin. He stood for only a split second; then he continued up to the stage for an impromptu jam session with the local band that was playing. Okay, so it was rather impressive, I must admit. They left the nightclub as quickly as they had arrived, leaving everyone in a fit of excitement. I was shocked when a dude in a black suit walked up to me and said, "Please accompany me to the limousine." I grinned and followed him. He opened the passenger door for me to go in. I glanced in, and it was Axl Rose.

I moved inside the limousine, directly in front of him. "You think you are hot shit, don't you?" I asked.

He just sat there with this smirk on his face and then said, "And I think you are ballsy." I laughed a bit as he autographed his name on a small piece of paper and handed it to me, grabbing my hand and pulling me close enough to whisper his

hotel and room number. I smiled at him while exiting the limousine. I rejoined my friends, and we left. Nope, I didn't join
him at the hotel, and I didn't regret it.

Keel

1985–1986

I think that sometimes we have mental blocks for a reason. And for whatever reason, I think that maybe we should respect it. But if I could make a guess of the reason why, it would be because there are a lot of games being played with one another's minds and also with one another's hearts. Sordid little games.

I really liked Marc, and I think he really liked me. He was absolutely good looking, and just a super easygoing guy. I do remember being together all day and ending up at the motel where they were staying, but we didn't do anything except just talk until I finally decided to leave. I remember leaving him in his room and then walking on the sidewalk toward my car when I heard a male calling out, "Now why are you leaving, pretty lady?" I quickly looked over to see Keel's other guitarist, Bryan. Why had I not noticed before that he was absolutely drop-dead gorgeous, with the longest, most beautiful flowing waves of blond hair? He was the most beautiful scammer I had ever seen. He walked straight over to me, taking me into a big hug.

"I just left Marc, and I was heading home," I said.

He had his arm draped over my shoulder as we walked together toward his room. "He's such a bore sometimes."

"Really now?" I peered at him with a slight grin.

He smiled at me. "Yeah, you should have been partying with us all along." I couldn't help but smile, thinking "such a smooth and very hot scammer." He opened the door to his room to reveal a room full of dudes drinking and lounging about; we even went to the bathroom to find some private space, but two guys were crashed out in the bathtub. He quietly closed the door. "Shhhh!"

We left the room and started walking to my car. "I really do need to go home." Bryan pinned me against the car, and we began kissing, and even though I was in heaven, all I could think about was feeling like I was betraying Marc, even though we hadn't done anything. I would have loved to stay with Bryan, but instead I figured the best choice was to leave.

Marc and I stayed in touch, writing to each other and eventually talking on the telephone. I wasn't sure when I would see him again. He was, however, becoming close friends with the guys in Pantera, and it didn't take too long before he was coming back to Texas to hang out with the guys and me too.

Everything seemed to be really good, and I don't think Marc ever found out about the little incident between Bryan and me. We spent the whole day hanging out together, but toward the end of the night I needed to get home. There was a big party at Darrell's house that night, and I didn't quite feel like being a part of it all, so I pulled up in front of Darrell's house. We sat there for a few minutes, talking and occasionally kissing, until he finally got out and went. This, technically, was the last time I would ever see Marc because at some point during the party Marc would have sex with one of my best friends. It's always fascinating how people believed that doing something like this wouldn't get back to me when it obviously always did; in fact, my phone was ringing within an hour of the betrayal. I won't lie—I was very hurt by Marc, and I had a monstrous red ass at my best friend, whom I would never reconcile with. I was angry at Marc too, because I really sort of believed that maybe the two of us were trying to build on something. Maybe I had it all wrong; he was a musician, and I didn't put much faith in them. I also couldn't help but wonder if Marc had found out I had spent some time with Bryan, and even though nothing happened, maybe he thought something did happen. I was thinking too much about it, so I just let it go.

I was hanging out with this chick one afternoon when she received a phone call from Marc, which wasn't unusual, since this chick handled a lot of business for Darrell and Pantera. When Marc found out I was there with her, he wanted to talk to me. I just shook my head no, then said, "Ask him how Bryan is doing."

That chick looked at me. "Whoa, that was mean."

I did regret the remark, but whatever damage was done was from both of our own doings. Unfortunately, nothing would ever be resolved, and we would never speak again.

Cyanide City

2008

had (thankfully) been out of the groupie business for a very long time. I was married to Doug in 1993. I had Amber in 1994. I had Zachary in 1997. My life of peace and normality was warmly accepted.

The thing you must remember about bliss is that it usually doesn't last. My fourteen-year-old-daughter Amber walked into the living room with a perplexed look on her face. "Mom, there's this band…" My mind panicked as I thought to myself, "Oh God! No! Not that!" She went on to explain that she had been talking over the internet to a band from New Zealand named Cyanide City. The band had been on tour in America when there was some sort of altercation between the band and the management, causing the management to abandon the band in Florida. This was absolutely unprofessional but equally atrocious because the members of this band were all underage. "So can you help them, Mom?" Amber asked.

I was outraged that a female in management would make such a poor decision and realistically place these boys in such peril. I didn't know how I could possibly help them. I didn't have the money to transport them to our home, where I could look after them. So I figured they were a band—why not use their abilities as musicians to get them to me? I knew nothing about the booking process, but with a little ingenuity and the use of the internet, I bet I could figure this out. What had I gotten myself into?

I worked diligently at the computer, researching rock night-clubs along the way: in Florida, Alabama, Mississippi, Louisiana, and East Texas. I emailed each location, writing "Urgent" in the subject line and then explaining the situation. Unbelievably, my efforts worked, and I began sitting up gigs for them with food and funds for them to make their trek a little easier. In the meantime, we were sitting on three round-trip airline tickets to Helsinki, Finland. Amber was really interested in a lot of European bands so we were going to a music festival called the Mama Trash Festival. So I was on a timeline in terms of getting the boys to the house before we left on our trip. It took them about a week and a half to make it to our home, and they were very relieved and tired. I put two of the boys in my daughter's bedroom and the other two boys in my son's bedroom. My kids would sleep in my bedroom while they were there. To say I spoiled my kids would be an understatement. My son was a huge fan of *Jackass* and *Wildboyz*, so I had designed his bedroom in that theme, with all sorts of props—there was a tree with limbs stretching across the ceiling, and there was even a tree house. The band argued over who would get to sleep in the top bunk. I was taking a huge risk in allowing four complete strangers to stay in my home with my family. I put a lot of trust in people, and I am usually a pretty good judge of character. They were just young boys, and I didn't feel too threatened. Besides, the boy who was sleeping in the top bunk of my son's room had his Bible with him, and he read from it every day.

I stocked the house with plenty of sandwich stuff and lots of soda pop. I gave the complete rundown of all the rules and regulations and how my house ran from day to day. My husband worked all night and slept all day, so they basically had the complete run of my home. My last words to them as I loaded my suitcases into the trunk of my car, pointing to them, were "Don't fuck it up!" The kids and I left for the airport.

While the kids and I enjoyed our two-and-a-half-week vacation with the chilling winds and metal music of Helsinki, Finland, the boys were taking care of my home, learning all about living in the United States, and having a few little adventures along the way.

The first few days went by without even a hiccup, and just when they were cruising along, an earthshaking (literally) Texas thunderstorm decided to scare the shit out of four unsuspecting boys. Now I don't know what kind of storms they had in New Zealand, but these boys thought the world was coming to an end. Okay, if you have never been through a Texas thunderstorm, it is an experience that one would never forget.

First, the air is so hot and heavy it is stifling.

Second, the cold air is moving fast and hits the hot air head on.

Third, the color of the sky turns from a light gray to a darker gray, then to an ominous greenish color.

Fourth, the normal rumbles of the thunder increase so hard you can literally feel your bones shaking.

Fifth, the lightning starts off with one thick bolt and morphs into twenty.

Sixth, the rain! Oh my goodness, the rain comes down so hard you are afraid that the roof won't hold.

Seventh, there are scary high winds that would cause things to fly through the air without a tornado.

Eighth, *then*, if you are still with me, we are going to throw ice cubes down on you. The cubes can grow to the size of baseballs that are being thrown at the velocity of a bullet from a gun.

And this is where you would have found the members of Cyanide City huddled under a huge office desk, fearing for their lives. The storm eventually did pass without any damage. Finally the boys felt safe enough to venture out from the safety of the desk into a house with no electricity, which in Texas translates to no air-conditioning. Now, they were going to wish they were dead.

Normally, if I ever needed help with a band, I would leave Debbie as an emergency contact, but in this instance I decided it would be best to leave Grandma Wanda as an emergency contact. She does live right across the street. Doug had slept through it all as usual, and they decided instead of waking up and poking the bear they would call Grandma Wanda. She turned on that southern-lady charm, subsequently calming their nerves and assuring them everything was going to be all right. In the meantime Doug had woken up and discovered the electricity was out, and he was going to sneak up on and scare the shit out of the boys. He leaped out yelling at the top of his lungs, sending the boys into a panic.

So I wasn't ever told what exactly happened at this point, but I am 100 percent sure Doug was laughing his ass off, and in between he probably shouted, "SHIT YOUR PANTS?"

And as I said, I can't say for sure because I wasn't there, but I would bet some pants were shat in.

While the members of Cyanide City stayed with us, they had to get used to a lot of different things they weren't familiar with. We lived very near an air force base, so there was a constant presence of fighter jets flying very low over our neighborhood. Trust me, if you aren't used to it, it can be very nerve racking. The boys told us they didn't have anything like that. The Blue Angels at the air force base would also practice their maneuvers right over our house, flying so low that you could see the pilots. When I was a little girl, I would stay at my nanie's house, and she lived right in the landing zone of the air force base, which housed at that time the largest airplane in existence, the B-52. It was so loud you had to cover your ears, and it rumbled the house so hard it would cause cracks on the ceiling and walls. Really scary!

My husband had his fun with the boys, but he was also very firm with them by making them pull their weight around the house while they were there. Our house is surrounded by huge oak trees, and every fall our yard is blanketed with layers of leaves, and we aren't very diligent about keeping up with the upkeep. So Doug put them to work raking and bagging leaves in the blistering Texas summer heat. Needless to say the boys were sunburned and very sore. Doug was very pleased with the results.

They had a lot of fun entertaining themselves by playing video games, playing the Sims, and playing pool. They found a huge box under my son's bed full of every Halloween costume he had ever worn, and let me tell you, that opened a whole barrel of fun. They shot a video blog in our house pretending MTV had dropped in on them. It was the funniest thing I had ever seen. I advise you to go check it out on Youtube: Cyanide City vblog 080424.

After almost three weeks abroad, the kids and I finally returned home. I was so thankful that my house was exactly as I had left it. I decided that it was time to show these boys a really good time as a thank-you for taking such good care of my home. It was definitely time for them to experience the infamous Rockstar Bar and be introduced to my dear friends Warren and Jay, who exuded true Texas hospitality. Cyanide City had the opportunity to play a set of music, and everyone went mad over them. After the partying an excess of drinking ensued well into the night, and again the boys were blindsided. At the end of the night, their faces were completely drawn on with Marks-A-Lots, and on the drive home, we literally had to tie belts around them so we could lean them out the van door so they could profusely vomit. Their recovery from the largest hangover they had ever experienced took a couple of days, about the same length of time the money from their parents arrived and before you know it they were board a bus to Los Angeles, California, and then take a flight home to New Zealand. We had all gotten so attached to them that we cried as their bus pulled out of sight. I was heartbroken because I didn't think we would ever see them again, but I would be wrong. The drummer's name was Jackson. My husband had nicknamed him Tito, but Jackson never understood why. I guess because he was the youngest member, the whole family had grown especially attached to him. We didn't realize the feeling was mutual. Jackson has been back to Texas to visit us numerous times for milestone events and just because he missed us. I do hope the visits continue for a very long time.

W.A.S.P./Damian

October 22, 1984
Reunion Arena

I wasn't necessarily a big W.A.S.P. fan, but our promoter friend set us up for the show with tickets and backstage passes. You know, you must keep up appearances backstage, keep your face fresh, because if you don't, your star could fade, and another pretty groupie face could take your place. W.A.S.P. was actually a seasoned band creating a big name for itself, a KISS-ish theatrical and gritty stage show, and its members were known for being really raunchy on and off the stage.

It isn't the headlining act this chapter revolves around; instead it revolves around a virtually unknown Wichita Falls, Texas, band by the name of Damian. After the show we went backstage to meet the band and get autographs, but other than that nothing out of the ordinary happened. Well, that was until I met the opening band, Damian. Its members were really nice and quite good looking. I immediately connected up with the guitarist, named Steve, and before we realized it, we had spent an inordinate amount of time together. We had spent so much time together that Steve's band had left without him. Yep, you heard that right. Damian left its guitarist with me. I am not entirely certain, but I'm not sure I would have taken too kindly to being left in a strange town. But anyway, this had never happened to me before, and there weren't many options left for me. We could have driven him to the next gig, we could have driven him home to Wichita Falls, Texas, or the most favored idea was that we could have a new roommate at our apartment, at least until he could arrange for someone to come and get him. I have said it so many times, but this shit only happens to us! The only other time something sort of like this happened to us was when Ozzy Osbourne's guitarist Jake E. Lee stayed a couple of days with Debbie, but even then the tour was over. Holy hell, it was two days of unadulterated sex between Debbie and Jake E. Lee. Did you ever wonder how many times you can fuck to Robin Trower's six-minute song "Caravan To Midnight"? We do!! Somehow Jake E. Lee's girlfriend got the telephone number to our apartment, and we had to endure weeks of threatening phone calls.

I was certain that Steve must have a girlfriend because he was being faithful, because he had no interest in sexual relations, only hugging and kissing, and after a few days cold showers weren't even consoling my pent-up sexual perversions. However, after a few days passed, his sister drove down from Wichita Falls to take him home. We stayed in touch for years, writing letters, exchanging pictures, and then it just gradually faded away. I don't know what happened to the band Damian or Steve, so wherever he is, I sure do wish him well.

Raven Lunatics

Raven, 1985 to present

Do you want to know which rock star I have shared the longest friendship with? That's an easy one! That would be Mr. John Gallagher from the metal maniacs themselves, Raven.

The first time we met was in early 1985, backstage at one of his concerts. I can't really explain it, except it was an instant connection. We bonded over our intense love of music, among other things. We went to eat at Denny's once, and I was sitting in between John and Mark. The two of them are from Newcastle, England, so their dialect was difficult to understand on its own, but since they were brothers, it was as if they had developed their own language. It didn't take me long at all until I could understand them just fine. I think what I loved the most about John and Mark was the very close bond they shared as brothers, but on top of that, they were the best of friends. It is enduring.

In the earlier years, John and I would try to see each other as often as we could. He would call even if they were just driving through. He would write to me and send me pictures, and one year he recorded himself on a cassette tape playing bass guitar for me. The highlight of the cassette tape was at the end, where he played "Happy Birthday," which meant so very much since it was my birthday.

It seemed like every time we saw each other, I felt more and more like just a member of the Gallagher family, but then everything changed. We both drifted off in different directions; I like to call it our "growing up and maturing" period of life. We both had gotten married and started families. I was so busy with being a wife, a mother of two children, and in charge of running a household. I didn't have time to think or even reminisce about the past. Around this period of time, a social network by the name of Facebook took the internet by storm, making it really easy to connect with just about anyone, and I joined in just like everyone else. I was able to talk to so many people that I had lost touch with throughout the years, and yes, I reconnected with John. We had the best time chatting about all the good times from our past, as well as where life had taken us. John was married too and had two children as well. We made a pact to try and see each other whenever we could, and since Raven was making a huge comeback with new generations of metalheads, getting to see each other was not that difficult because the band toured relentlessly as usual. It was incredible because I was able to introduce my children to Raven but also to John and Mark.

So let me explain to you exactly what type of guy John Gallagher really is. Both of my kids are in college, working toward their forever careers, and so my son approached me with a dilemma. The class, World Culture, issued a project where he had to conduct an interview with someone who had lived in a different country and moved to the United States, explaining all the changes and differences the person would face. I had no idea what to do until I started going through my Facebook and saw John's name. I hated to contact John because this man is always busy working, making music, and touring. But when I messaged him, he dropped everything and made himself available, and for over an hour, my son asked John questions. John answered all my son's questions, gave great answers, told priceless stories, and provided priceless information. The personal attention John gave and all the hard work my son put into a stellar paper garnered him a grade of 110 percent, the top grade. My son said the professor was pretty psyched when my son told him who he did the interview with. It seems the professor is a huge fan of Raven.

I cherish John as a very dear friend and I suspect he and I will remain friends for the rest of our lives.

John Gallagher & Linda

"You're Booked!"

2008–2010

My experience booking gigs for Cyanide City led me into starting a new business of band management and booking: Heaven & Hell Productions. My husband even thought that with all my past experiences, dealing with bands would come pretty easy. We had become friends with a Santa Cruz, California, band called Dirty Penny, and this band had a colorful manager by the name of Chilli. He was very experienced in the business, and he wanted to work with me, so we allowed him to move in with us so we could create this successful business. Chilli was one of the most unique people I had ever met—even with my past history of characters, no one came close to Chilli. He had all these catchphrases that I am sure are copyrighted under his name. When it was time to pack up and leave a location, he would say, "Tighten it up!!" When a member of the band was spending too much time with a groupie, he would yell to that person, "HIT IT! Don't babysit it!!!" And of course one of the all-time favorites was "What's up, slut? You wanna get cut?"

My son, Zachary, was eleven years old at the time, and he looked up to Chilli, and I wasn't exactly proud that he would act just like Chilli, spouting off band talk like he had done it his whole life. One day the band Dirty Penny went to a large department store and bought Zachary a hat that matched Chilli's exactly.

In the beginning we took on so many bands, and we rapidly booked gigs, some with success and others not so much. Unfortunately the work relationship between Chilli and me soured, and we ceased working together. I should have stopped right then and there, but my husband and I saw dollar signs, and I continued booking. I guess you could say it was the most fun job I ever had, and I was pretty good at it.

I started letting bands stay at my house rather than some seedy motel. I had only two rules; no drugs in the house and no groupies. It was a nice little hideout and rest for them.

I had this precious little dog we named Winston, and one night we were getting ready to leave for the gig when all of a sudden Winston started walking by me but backward, with his head all distorted. "What the fuck is wrong with my dog!?!?" I thought. At first I was blaming the band, thinking Winston got a hold of a quaalude or something, but the band members swore that they didn't have any. My husband stayed home to watch him while I got the band to the gig. While we were gone, Winston barfed up a huge marijuana bud; then he was just fine. So after all that, it was my husband's fault because the marijuana was his.

We had another dog named Pockets, and this dog was a complete legend with everyone. He was very old and we would joke with all the bands that when he died we were going to have him stuffed. This one band freaked out so badly that they wrote a song called "Don't Stuff Pockets!"

I was able to tour all over the United States, and most importantly I got to take my kids with me. They were able to experience so many magical things, such as swimming off the shores of South Carolina, seeing the history of our government in Washington, DC, watching Amish buggies ride by, riding the subway, and peering off the Empire State Building in New York City. We had so much fun along the way, like taking street cones from each state, and yes, they are different. Band members running around with "Wet floor" signs on their heads, beautiful lead singers being attacked by crickets at a service station in the middle of the night, another lead singer running around in his underwear screaming, "I'm looking for Gothic chicks!" And we cannot forget this phrase from Paul: "Extreme sitting!"

I was able to attend SXSW in Austin, Texas. I also was able to meet some amazing musicians, such as Michael Monroe from Helsinki's Hanoi Rocks and the legendary Roger Daltrey from the Who. I worked with some bands that were unbelievable human beings and loaded with unbounding talent, such as Two Choices, The Faded, Vains of Jenna, Staci Grim, and Eye. But as you know, with all the good, you will undoubtedly have bad apples. This type of band used everything that was good and happy, including my heart, and stomped it into the ground. I did not deserve the amount of abuse that I endured from one specific lead singer. So in 2010 I took this band to the airport for their flight back to England. I had given the members of this band every ounce of support, and I even put forth one thousand dollars of my own money to promote them. They walked away without a goodbye, a simple thank-you, or one penny in return for all the work I did for them. I was gutted.

You know I don't need no wannabe rock star treating me like shit, so guess what?

I QUIT!

Conclusion

When I was younger, my parents used to laugh and say, "If you can't find Linda, just follow the little paper trail, and you'll find her." They definitely weren't wrong. I'm sixty years old, and you will still find that same paper trail. My mom used to buy me these really cool hardcover calendar books. I got a new one every Christmas. Throughout my life I would write down everything that would happen to me in the little squares provided for writing down appointments, birthdays, and so on. I have stacks and stacks of them packed away. I also have boxes full of probably millions of little notes about every minuscule thing that happened to me in my life. I have been writing projects my entire life, whether it was poetry, fan fiction, stories, or of course, in my later years, my memoir. It has always been my lifelong dream to have my words written down so they will be remembered forever.

Is It Just Me?

Well, here I am—
Lying here with you.
I thought last year
You told me we were through
Sometimes I don't understand
The way you are
You always keep coming back for more
Is it just me
Or do you just need it?
Well, here I am—
Saying goodbye to you,
For the last time once again
I'll always be there, always true
Sometimes I just can't understand
The way I am
I'm always bouncing back for more
Is it just me?
Or do I just need it?
  —Written by Linda Temple, 1984

Scamming

Backstage; this is our place
Finish the whole tour
And we still want more
We're scamming!
Hanging around in the dressing room.
How much metal have we consumed?
Out on the road
In our lace and leathered daze
Scamming! Scamming!
Making it from day to day
Because we love living this way
You know they'll never understand
And they say there's no future
In electric guitars
And the boys in the band
We're scamming!
We live fast!
We live it hard!
We walk on the edge
Trying to hold on
And not fall off
Scamming!
And we will always last!
   —Written by Linda Temple, 1985

Trash!

I'm sick of
Your fucking one-night stands—
And your—
Wait until next year.
There's not a thing called love—
And I guess there never was...
My past experiences should show
You can't love a free bird
But I always thought there was a way
Or something would turn out right
Funny, it seems—it never does.
Here I am!
Trash my heart!
Take all you can!
Lovin' you—
Was all my mistake—
Caught in a scam!
You fly into my life
And my life
For a couple of days
Or even shorter a time.
Love me; promise me dreams
(that won't come true)
I should have already learned and know
That you were not all mine

Here I am!
Trash my heart!
Take all you can!
Lovin' you
Was all my mistake
Caught in a scam!
   —Written by Linda Temple, 1985

List of All the Concerts
I Have Been To

1970s

Sept. 19, 1973: ZZ Top, Tarrant County Convention Center

Apr. 3, 1977: Jackson Five/Wild Cherry, Tarrant County Convention Center

July 3, 1977: Alice Cooper, Tarrant County Convention Center

Aug. 19, 1977: Steve Miller, Tarrant County Convention Center

Sept. 4, 1977: KISS/Styx, Tarrant County Convention Center

Dec. 2, 1978: Aerosmith/Nazareth/Liberation, Tarrant County Convention Center

June 20, 1979: Journey/AC|DC/New England, Tarrant County Convention Center

Oct. 23, 1979: KISS/Jon Butcher, Tarrant County Convention Center

1980

Mar. 21, 1980: Rock and Roll Marathon. Frank Marino and Mahogany Rush/Humble Pie/Angel/Mother's Finest, Tarrant County Convention Center

Mar. 22, 1980: ZZ Top/Expect No Quarter, Tarrant County Convention Center

Oct. 17, 1980: Kansas

Nov. 25, 1980: Van Halen autograph-signing party,
Peaches Record and Tapes Dallas, Texas

1981

Apr. 12, 1981: Rush/Max Webster, Tarrant County
Convention Center

June 5, 1981: Ozzy Osbourne/Motörhead, Will Rogers
Coliseum

Nov. 7, 1981: Journey/Loverboy, Reunion Arena

Nov. 19, 1981: Blackfoot/Def Leppard, Wintergarden

1982

Aug. 21, 1982: Queen/Billy Squier, Reunion Arena

Dec. 26, 1982: Aerosmith/Rose Tattoo, Reunion Arena

1983

Feb. 18, 1983: Sammy Hagar/Night Ranger, Reunion Arena

Mar. 9, 1983: KISS/Plasmatics/Riot/Vandenburg, Reunion
Arena

Apr. 17, 1983: Berlin, the Ritz

Aug. 14, 1983: Cheap Trick, the Ritz

Sept. 16, 1983: Quiet Riot/Queensrÿche/Axe, Bronco Bowl

Sept. 30, 1983: ZZ Top/Albert King, Reunion Arena

Dec. 3, 1983: Mötley Crüe/Kick Axe, Bronco Bowl

1984

Feb. 16, 1984: Ozzy Osbourne/Mötley Crüe, Reunion Arena

July 15, 1984: Van Halen/The Velcros, Reunion Arena

July 24, 1984: Twisted Sister/Ratt, Reunion Arena

Sept. 9, 1984: Sammy Hagar/Krokus, Reunion Arena

Sept. 26, 1984: KISS/Wendy O. Williams, Reunion Arena

Oct. 21, 1984: Quiet Riot/Whitesnake/Helix, Reunion Arena

Oct. 22, 1984: W.A.S.P./Damien, Reunion Arena

Oct. 28, 1984: Quiet Riot/Whitesnake/Helix, Ector
Coliseum, Amarillo, Texas

Nov. 14, 1984: John Waite/Scandal, Dallas County
Convention Center

Nov. 18, 1984: Dio/Dokken, Reunion Arena

Nov. 28, 1984: Mercyful Fate/Motörhead/Exciter, Palladium
Arena

Dec. 13, 1984: Aerosmith/Black 'N Blue/Stone Fury,
Reunion Arena

Dec. 22, 1984: W.A.S.P., Arcadia Theater

Dec. 30, 1984: Cheap Trick, the Ritz

1985

Jan. 25, 1985: Deep Purple/Giuffria, Reunion Arena

Jan. 26, 1985: KISS/Queensrÿche, Austin County
Convention Center, Austin, Texas

Jan. 29, 1985: KISS/Queensrÿche, Reunion Arena

Feb. 27, 1985: Metallica/Armored Saint, Reunion Arena

Feb. 28, 1985: Metallica/Armored Saint, Cardi's,
Houston, Texas

Mar. 1–2, 1985: Spent with Metallica, Houston, Texas

Apr. 5, 1985: Steve Marriott/Lightning, Joe's Garage, Fort Worth, Texas

Apr. 6, 1985: Raven/Lightning, Dallas, Texas

Apr. 13, 1985: Spent with John Gallagher, Dallas, Texas

Apr. 30, 1985: Krokus/Accept/Coney Hatch, Dallas County Convention Center

May , 1985: Mama's Boys/Pantera, Joe's Garage, Fort Worth, Texas

June 27, 1985: Yngwie Malmsteen/Rising Force/Talas, Dallas County Convention Center

June 28, 1985: Spent with Rising Force, Dallas, Texas

Aug. 20, 1985: Accept/Keel/Y&T, Bronco Bowl

Oct. 1, 1985: AC|DC/Y&T, Reunion Arena

Oct. 2, 1985: Mötley Crüe/Y&T, Reunion Arena

Oct. 16, 1985: Iron Butterfly/Mannekin, Savvy's, Fort Worth, Texas

Oct. 23, 1985: Poison, the Ritz

Oct. 30, 1985: Sting, Reunion Arena

Dec. 4, 1985: KISS/Black 'N Blue, Reunion Arena

Dec. 7, 1985: Stryper/Heaven, Bronco Bowl

1986

Feb. 28, 1986: Aerosmith/Y&T, Reunion Arena

Mar. 17–18, 1986: Spent with Marc Ferrari (Keel), Fort Worth, Texas

Apr. 4, 1986: Ozzy Osbourne/Metallica, Reunion Arena

Apr. 20, 1986: Ted Nugent/Raven/King Kobra, Reunion Arena

June 18, 1986: Poison

June 27, 1986: Judas Priest/Dokken, Reunion Arena

Aug. 5, 1986: AC|DC/Queensrÿche, Reunion Arena

Aug. 8, 1986: Loudness/Cinderella/Poison, Reunion Arena

Sept. 30, 1986: Huey Lewis and the News/Duane Eddy and the Cruisers, Reunion Arena

Oct. 2, 1986: Mötley Crüe, Reunion Arena

Oct. 25, 1986: Motörhead/Wendy O. Williams/Cro-Mags/ Scratch Aide

Nov. 21, 1986: David Lee Roth/Cinderella, Reunion Arena

Dec. 2, 1986: Lizzy Borden, Savvy's Nightclub, Fort Worth, Texas

Dec. 4, 1986: KISS/W.A.S.P., Reunion Arena

Dec. 14, 1986: Bret Michaels party at the Hard Rock Cafe, Dallas, Texas. Met Weird Al Yankovic

Dec. 16, 1986: Ratt/Poison, Tarrant County Convention Center

1987

Feb. 20, 1987: W.A.S.P./Slayer/Raven, State Fair Coliseum

Feb. 22, 1987: Ratt/Poison, Tarrant County Convention Center

Apr. 10, 1987: Rigor Mortis, Arcadia Theater, Dallas, Texas

May 23, 1987: Anthrax/Firstsryche, Cain's Ballroom, Tulsa, Oklahoma

June 30, 1987: Anthrax/Metal Church, Bronco Bowl

Dec. 4, 1987: Alice Cooper/Guns N' Roses, Reunion Arena

1988

Feb. 27, 1988: KISS/Ted Nugent, Reunion Arena

Mar. 11, 1988: L.A. Guns/Uncle Sam, Tommy's on Canton, Dallas, Texas

May 24, 1988: Dirty Looks, Tommy's on Canton, Dallas, Texas

June 3, 1988: Yngwie Malmsteen/Lita Ford/Black 'N Blue, Bronco Bowl

1989

Nov. 4, 1988: Billy Squier (Strange event with Jimmy Crespo), Bronco Bowl

1990s

July 28, 1991: Operation Rock & Roll. Judas Priest/Alice Cooper/Motörhead/Dangerous Toys/Metal Church, Starplex

Jan. 24, 1992: The Cult, State Fair Coliseum

May 21, 1994: Doyle Bramhall, Caravan of Dreams, Fort Worth, Texas

Mar. 18, 1995: Page/Plant, Reunion Arena

2002

Sept. 6, 2002: Dio/Scorpions/Deep Purple, Smirnoff Arena

2003

Aug. 13, 2003: Dio/Iron Maiden/Motörhead, Smirnoff Arena

2007

Feb. 27, 2007: Three Inches of Blood/The 69 Eyes/
Palladium/Cradle of Filth

Mar. 18, 2007: Cute Is What We Aim For/Rookie of the
Year/Self Against City/Circa Survive, Ridglea Theater

July 2, 2007: The 69 Eyes/Wednesday 13/Night Kills the Day

July 5, 2007: To/Die/For, Dreamworld Complex, Fort
Worth, Texas

Aug. 4, 2007: Projekt Revolution. Linkin Park/My Chemical
Romance/HIM/Mindless Self Indulgence/Saosin/Taking
Back Sunday, Smirnoff Music Centre, Dallas, Texas

Oct. 22, 2007: Serj Tankian/Saul Williams, Granada Theater

Oct. 27, 2007: Mushroomhead/Marazene, the Rockyard,
Fort Worth, Texas

Nov. 20, 2007: HIM/Bleeding Through, South Side
Ballroom, Dallas, Texas

Dec. 9, 2007: Death by Decibels Tour. Malevolent Creation/
Cattle Decapitation/Light This City/ Veil of Maya/
Abigail Williams, Ridglea Theater, Fort Worth, Texas

2008

Apr. 18, 2008: Trash Fest. Andy McCoy and Hanoi Rocks/
Anzi Destruction/Gemini Five/Violent Divine/Dope
Stars Inc./Sexy Death/Deathstars/Private Line/Iconcrash,
Gloria, Helsinki, Finland

July 12, 2008: Rocklahoma, Pryor, Oklahoma
*Huge storm came in and we left

Aug. 30, 2008: Rock the Bayou. Sammy Hagar/Lita Ford/
    Dokken/Great White/Enuff Z'Nuff/BulletBoys/Steven
    Adler, Pryor, Oklahoma
Dec. 4, 2008: Gwar, Palladium Ballroom

2009
Jan. 18, 2009: Combichrist/Black Light Burns/Retard-o-bot,
    Granada Theater

2010
Apr. 29, 2010: HIM/We Are the Fallen/Dommin/Drive A,
    South Side Ballroom
June 25, 2010: Roger Daltrey (from the Who), Stiefel
    Theatre, Salina, Kansas
July 16, 2010: Rookie of the Year/School Boy Humor/TBA/
    The After Party

2014
Vans Warped Tour, Gexa Pavilion
Oct. 30, 2014: Devil's Night with Richie Ramone,
    Dallas, Texas

Random Bands I Have Seen

Acey Slade

Andy McCoy

Anzi Destruction

Assassin

Bad Candy

Bam Margera

Barbie-Q-Barbies

Battalion

Bellicose

Blackstar

Bowling for Soup

Brunette

Bugs Henderson

Carmine Appice

Chastity

Chaza Retta

CKY

Crashdïet

Damaged Dolls

Deathstars

Diamond Romeo
   (Brooks and Amo)

Die So Fluid

Dirty Blonde

Dope Stars Inc.

Eruption (Jeff)

EYE

The Faded

Gammacide

Gemini Five

Grim Reaper

Gypsy Pistoleros

Hammer Witch

HIM

Impact

Intimate Acts (Steve)

Jesse Valo

Kill Hannah

Kodi Lee

Lic

Lightning

Lillian Axe

L.O.U.D.

Malice

Michael Monroe

Mistress

Molly Maguires

Morbid Scream

Naked Zoo
Nasty Habits
Nice Brothers
Onyx
Psychostick
Razor White
Ricky Lynn Gregg
RipLaff
Rotting Corpse
 (Rodney E.)
Savvy
Sex Slaves
Sexy Death
Sheer Threat
Shock Tu
The 69 Eyes
The 69 Sins
Solinger

Sonic Roots
Stereo Junkies
Stiff
Sweet Savage
Talon
Tight Squeeze
TNA
Tunes of Dawn
Vains of Jenna
Valentino
Velvet 69
Violent Divine
Vizion
Warbeast
Warlord (Ricky C.)
WhiskeyDick
Wrathchild
The Zoo

About the Author

Linda Chadwick is a 60-year-old wife (of over 30 years), mother (to two grown children) and a pet mommy to many fur babies. She has been a lifelong resident of Texas. Her husband is recently retired, and she is enjoying her new time with him. She has always loved every facet of music. She has an intense love of writing and has dreamed of being published since she was 6 years old. She is an avid collector of antiques and has owned her own antique store. She is funny, which you will see reflected in her writing. She explains that she has many more books to come.

She has been awarded a Literary Award from The Fort Worth Poetry Society.

Milton Keynes UK
Ingram Content Group UK Ltd.
UKHW040633090224
437425UK00003B/45